Coorg And Its Rajahs

By an Officer
Formerly in the Service of
His Highness, Veer Rajunder Wadeer,
Erstwhile Rajah of Coorg

Low Price Publications

Low Price Publications
2015

First Published 1857
Reprinted in **LPP** 2015

ISBN 10: 81-7536-555-2
ISBN 13: 978-81-7536-555-1

Published by
Low Price Publications
A-6, 2nd Floor, Nimri Commercial Centre,
Ashok Vihar Phase 4, Delhi 110052 (INDIA)
tel.: +91-11-27302453 fax.: +91-11-47061936
url: www.LPPindia.com e-mail: info@LPPindia.com

Printed at
D.K. Fine Art Press Pvt. Ltd.
Delhi

PRINTED IN INDIA

COORG

AND ITS RAJAHS.

BY AN OFFICER

FORMERLY IN THE SERVICE OF

HIS HIGHNESS

VEER RAJUNDER WADEER,

RAJAH OF COORG.

LONDON:

JOHN BUMPUS, 158, OXFORD STREET.

M.DCCC.LVII.

DEDICATION.

TO HIS HIGHNESS VEER RAJUNDER WADEER,
RAJAH OF COORG.

HONOURED PRINCE,

HAVING, ere the "evil day" had arrived, received from your Highness many proofs of kindness, condescension, and generosity, I beg permission to dedicate the following narrative to you, not only as a mark of my sincere gratitude, but also as a token of my admiration of the philosophic fortitude and dignified patience with which your Highness has borne alike the wrongs of the oppressor and the aspersions of the slanderer.

I have the honour to be,

Honoured Prince,

Your Highness's Most Obedient and Most Grateful Servant,

THE AUTHOR.

LONDON, *May*, 1857.

COORG AND ITS RAJAHS.

MIDWAY on the Malabar coast of Cis-Gangetic India, between Mangalore and Cannanore, is the port of Bakull. If a straight line be drawn therefrom into the interior, it will touch Seringapatam, and the hill country which intersects it is Coorg. This Raj is bounded on the north by Mysore; on the south, by the Collectorate of Malabar; on the east, by Mysore; and on the west, by Malabar and Canara: but before its subjugation by the British, in 1834, it was more extensive. Coorg lies between N. lat. 11°. 56′ and 12°. 45′, and E. long. 75°. 25′ and 76°. 13′; its area, consequently, being about 1420 square miles. The longest line that can be drawn through it from north to south, measures 60 miles; and from east to west, 35 miles. The lowest parts of Coorg are not less than 3000 feet above the sea; its highest peaks, which rise to a height of 5682 and 5781 feet, have a full view of the Indian Ocean, though at a distance of 40 or 50 miles.

The principal river is the Kaveri, which rises in the eastern side of the Western Ghauts. Many streams and torrents flow into it during its course eastward into Mysore, of which the principal are the Soornavaty or Haringhee, and the Lechman Teert. During the dry season, the Kaveri is reduced to very insignificant dimensions, having scarcely either breadth or depth. The minor streams intersecting Coorg vary only in size, which depends upon the length of their course. They swell in the early part of June, and flow with a violent and boisterous rapidity till October, when they gradually diminish and become placid. During the western monsoon, every rivulet roughens into a wild torrent.

The temperature in Coorg is low: a circumstance easily accounted for, not only by the great elevation of the country, but also by the proximity of the ocean to the south-west and west, and the prevalence of the winds from those points. Owing to these causes, the thermometer seldom rises higher than 74°, or sinks below 60°, in the open air. During the dry season, the range is a little higher, the daily extremes being from 62° or 63° to 68° or 70°. The hottest months are those of April and May, but even then the nights are cool. The monsoon, which commences in June, continues during July, August, and September. This is the rainy season, and the air is in these three months so loaded with vapour that the sun is rarely visible; yet, notwithstanding this humidity, the equality of temperature renders rheumatic affections, coughs, colds, &c. extremely rare. Not so with asthmatic affections, chronic diseases of the liver, and dysenteric complaints, which are, of course, exacerbated by the rarified and often cold and damp air.

The country presents a succession of hills and valleys, placed at a medium elevation between the sultry plains and the tempestuous tops of mountains. Ravines and chasms, into whose abysses the solar ray seldom penetrates, tell the tale of violent and wide-spread disruptions, and awaken in the mind of the traveller mingled emotions of awe and admiration. The prevailing geological formations are primitive. Large masses of felspar, of a cream colour, partially decomposed, and in the state of what is called porcelain clay, are also of frequent occurrence.

The whole of the eastern boundary—that is, in the direction of Mysore—exhibits an almost uninterrupted and impervious forest. Here the underwood becomes very thick, and the bamboo frequently rises to the height of 60 feet. In the jungle roam elephants, tigers, chitas or hunting leopards, tiger-cats, a few bears, wild dogs, bisons, elks, several species of deer, wild boars, hares, and monkeys. Of the feathered tribes, eagles, hawks, parrots, woodcocks, snipes, pigeons, and the rhinoceros bird, or buceros, are the most common. Reptiles are but few, among which may be mentioned the deadly cobra di capello, several varieties of snakes, and a few alligators.

Coorg possesses many antiquities, but the most interesting ones are certain earth fortifications or redoubts, called by the natives *kunnidegs*. These are generally from 15 to 25 feet high, with a ditch in front of 10 feet deep by 8 or 10 wide; and being in many places double, triple, or quadruple, their linear extent cannot be less than between 500 and 600 miles. The tradition respecting these works is, that in times of which there exist no historical records, the people lived in a state of general warfare, chief fighting against chief, and nada (district) against nada. Whatever, however, may be the credit due to this explanation, certain it is that the antiquity of these works is evidently very great, as enormous trees, which must have been the growth of centuries, are still found on many parts of the walls.

The country has, for ages, been inhabited by a dozen tribes, of which the highest in rank is that of the Kaveri Brahmin, and the lowest that of slaves: the intermediate ones being those who exercise trades or follow agricultural pursuits.

The inhabitants of Coorg are Nairs, and, consequently, Brahminists of the Sudra caste. They are a bold and active race of mountaineers, and, though once of lawless and predatory habits, are much attached to their chiefs. "The men of Coorg," says Thornton,[1] "are a handsome, athletic race, usually above the middle size, and, with scarcely any excep-

[1] *Gazetteer of India*, Art. Coorg.

tions, well limbed. The women are not so tall in proportion, but are well made and well looking, though rather coarse, but fair in comparison with the men. Both sexes are laborious, and industrious in the practice of agriculture, their main and almost exclusive employment; except that the men shoot and hunt, partly to destroy animals injurious to their crops, and partly for the produce of the sport. They are well clad, the men wearing a turban, and a gown reaching to the feet, and being girt round the waist with a shawl or handkerchief, to which they attach the formidable Nair knife. The women wear a loose cotton wrapper, reaching from the shoulders to the knees, and a small white cloth tied round the head. Both sexes daily, after labour, wash the whole body in warm water."

A principal cause of the strong and vigorous constitution of the Coorgs, which has been greatly aided by the excellent climate and open-air life of the people, is their custom of late marriages. In former times, the Coorg men used to marry when they had attained the age of thirty; and even now they do so at a comparatively ripe age. But they have a strange and, to us, disgusting custom, a kind of marriage communism within the family. The wives of the brothers of one house are considered as common property; and, as the juniors successively marry their wives in turn, these are common also to all the brothers. The children, consequently, are rather children of the family, or of the mother, than of the acknowledged father.

It is not very difficult to conjecture how such a custom may have taken root among this people. In warlike races, especially when under the influence of pantheistic ideas, the clannish feeling and the family spirit often predominate over and almost absorb individual consciousness and personal rights. Among the Coorgs, the family property descends, accordingly, not so much from father to son, as from generation to generation, the oldest member acting as head of the house. The general state of warfare, which we have described above as existing in ancient times, very probably had also some share in originating this custom, for the people must soon have been exterminated under such a state of things, had not a remedy been found for the evil by the surviving brothers of a family becoming the rightful husbands of the widows; and thus a second and undiminished generation might rise, in time, to supply the place of the fallen.

The festivals of the Coorgs are few in number. The Kaveri Habba (festival), and the Huttari or Huddari Habba, are the two principal festive seasons. The former has reference to the river, the most ancient object, no doubt, of Coorg worship; the latter to the earth, which, by its rich harvests, gives food and plenty to the chosen race. A Baghavati festival is observed all over Coorg, in the months preceding the monsoon. After the sowing season, generally, at the first break of the monsoon, the Kailmutter, the festival of arms, is celebrated by the youths and men of Coorg.

The Coorgs are represented by the people of the plains as a fierce, irascible, and revengeful race, not easily to be managed. They have always been an unlettered nation. To the present day, they are very ignorant, and, consequently, superstitious. The prevailing worship is that of demons and departed spirits. Charms and sorceries abound all over the country. Disease among men and cattle is readily ascribed to the maledictions and witchcraft of enemies. The dead annoy the living, and demand sacrifices and other atonements.

As to the population of Coorg, the last official census was made in 1839-40, when it was stated that there were in Coorg 17,096 Coorgs, and 64,341 people of other castes. The Coorgs are the principal landholders of the country lying to the south and west of Mercara. They have, from ancient times, been lords of the soil, and still enjoy great privileges. They pay only five per cent. of the produce of their land, while other lands are assessed at ten, fifteen, and twenty per cent.

Coorg produces an annual rice harvest of the value of upwards of seven lacs of rupees, or £70,000. The Rajahs used to make 80,000 rupees annually by the sale of cardamoms, which, like sandal-wood, were considered Government property. The whole net revenue of Coorg amounted, in 1853, to 126,000 rupees. The manufactures of the country are confined to a coarse kind of blanket, which forms part of the dress of the common people; the cotton cloths which they use are all imported.

The chief towns of Coorg are Merkara, Somwarpet, Verajenderpett, and Periapatam; the latter was, in former times, the capital, but, after the growth of the Mysore power, the Rajahs lived at Mercara, a place more protected by the mountains. This town, which is in 12°. 26′ N. lat. and 75°. 30′ E. long., being about twenty miles north from the Pondicherrum Pass, stands surrounded by an amphitheatre of hills. The fort is a pentagon, with towers and bastions. Within was the Rajah's palace, which was handsomely furnished in the European style.

Feudalism, very similar to that which obtained in Europe during the middle ages, appears to have prevailed, in ancient times, throughout Hindostan. Its native princes, with the title of universal monarchs, seem to have been invested only with a delegated power, voluntarily conferred, by a numerous and powerful band of subordinate sovereigns. The very title of Maharajah, or Rajah of Rajahs, which the nominal head of the vast empire of Hindostan anciently bore, evidently implies no more than a kind of feudal jurisdiction over chieftains possessing absolute dominion in their own territories, but contributing a stipulated sum and force or contingent to support the grandeur of the imperial throne; and, on great occasions, ranging themselves, with succours proportionate to the extent and population of their respective dominions, under the banners of one supreme chief. Thus, in ancient times, the Rajahs of Coorg, who are mentioned by Ferishtah (a Persian historian of the seventeenth century) as being independent sovereigns as far back as the year 1538, were feudatories of the Ikkeri

Government; and when Hyder Ali, having taken Ikkeri, incorporated that kingdom in his growing dominions, he considered himself the liege lord of Coorg; it is true that he was, for a long time, foiled in his assertion of suzerainty, but he at last succeeded, by dint of force and fraud, in coercing the refractory hill chiefs into a state of vassalage, and enforcing the payment of tribute.

It was not till about this time that Coorg became well known to Europeans; and, indeed, the English may be said to have been first acquainted with it in the Mysore wars with Hyder Ali and Tippoo Sultan, in which the Company were engaged from the years 1782 to 1798. In the first of these wars, Hyder Ali, victorious everywhere, ravaged the Carnatic, besieged Madras, and had nearly expelled the English from South India, when the Company sued for peace. In 1790, when the war broke out with Tippoo Sultan, an enemy scarcely less formidable and more implacable than his father Hyder, the Company possessed not a foot of territory along the whole line of the Malabar coast, save a few struggling commercial factories, which they contemplated abandoning, from inability to defend them singly against the overwhelming power of the Sultan. With these exceptions, this prince was master of all the coast provinces lying between the Western Ghauts and the sea; he held every pass but one leading from those provinces to the high table land of Mysore; and possessed all the intervening country stretching from these mountains to the Carnatic, one solitary spot alone excepted. In that vast extent of country, reaching nearly from sea to sea, the solitary spot the Sultan did not possess, and the only pass he could not command and bar against the English, were the Principality of Coorg, seated on the very crest of the lofty mountains looking down upon Malabar and the western coast, and situated near the heart of Tippoo's dominions; and the Ghaut, or pass, leading directly from Coorg to the Company's chief factory of Tellicherry, and thus communicating with the sea, and with the Company's western stronghold, Bombay. This defile was, in the hands of such a people, a key to military operations in the country over which Hyder Ali had established his dominion. That the possession of Coorg was of the utmost importance to him, will still further appear, when it is considered that the Mysore country is guarded by a range of mountains rising to a surprising height, and opposing to the eastern borders of the Carnatic a mural front, having Ghauts or passes in various directions. These Ghauts, from which the whole chain of mountains derives its name, give entrance into the lofty, fertile, and populous plains of boundless view, which they support as buttresses do some immense and extensive terrace. The Mysore country, being at least 2000 feet higher than the level of the Carnatic, is thence called the table land; the ascent to which is not to be accomplished, even by a single traveller, without the fatiguing labour of many hours. The pathways up the Ghauts are worked by the hand of man, along the deep-worn channel of some rapid torrent, or skirting the hollow ravines and winding excavations which have formed themselves on the face of this mountain precipice; and, in many of these passes, the obstructions of art, as well as their natural ones, are opposed to the progress of an invading army. It may well, then, be imagined that Hyder Ali made many and desperate attempts to become master of Coorg, and thus to gain the means of extending his territories on the other side of the Ghauts; but he was continually unsuccessful, until feuds in the family of the Rajah came to his assistance. By the treachery of a relative, the whole family was surprised and carried off to Seringapatam, and there placed in a strict and severe captivity.

In the year 1780, Sing Rajunder, who had thus betrayed the Horamale branch of the family into the hands of Hyder Ali, died, leaving a natural son, Appajii, and two sons by his queen, Veer Rajunder and Sing Rajunder. The former was then seventeen years old, the latter still of tender age. Hyder Ali, who had destroyed the entire Horamale family, now declared himself guardian of the two young Coorg princes, and appointed a Brahmin, Subarasaga, who had formerly been in the service of the Coorg Rajahs, Mamaldar or Governor of Coorg. In the same year, he led his army against Arcot. The Coorgs were indignant at the seizure of their princes and the ascendency of the Brahmin, and, in the monsoon of 1782, broke out into open insurrection. No sooner was Hyder Ali informed of this, than he ordered the princes to be secured in Garuru, a Mysore fort; the Coorgs again flew to arms, and swept the Mussulmans from the country.

Hyder Ali died in 1782, and was succeeded by his son Tippoo, who, in 1784, having reduced Mangalore, marched through Coorg, on his way back to Seringapatam, and compromised matters with the insurgents. The young Coorg princes were kept prisoners at Periyaputtana. Before the lapse of a year, the Coorgs rose again and defeated a force of 15,000 men sent against them from Seringapatam. Tippoo's policy and zeal for his religion appear to have led him to expect that these warlike Hindoo tribes might be subdued like wild animals and tamed by violence, and that, by subjecting the Coorgs and Nairs to the rites of his creed, they would be the sooner reconciled to his yoke. Taking advantage, therefore, of this last formidable resistance to his authority, he marched against them with his whole force, the Coorgs retreating before him into the depths of their forests, which appeared almost inaccessible. Having, however, divided his whole army into detachments, which formed a complete circle round the unhappy fugitives, and closing in upon them as huntsmen do in pursuit of game, he at length penetrated into their most secret haunts, and carried off several thousands of victims to undergo the abhorred punishments of circumcision and captivity. The rank of the young Rajah did not save him from like treatment: he was made a Mussulman, and enrolled among the Chelas (corps of slaves); and, though strictly guarded, had the nominal command of a battalion, at the time he made his escape.

In December, 1788, Veer Rajunder Wadeer, by the help of his Coorg partisans, escaped from Periyaputtana with his family, for whom he obtained a refuge at Kurchi, a sequestered spot in Kiggadnad, near the sources of the Lakshmanatirtha river.[1] Although the greater part of his subjects were groaning in exile, he nevertheless found, in the depths of the woody recesses, a band of freemen who rallied round him with enthusiastic ardour. By a series of exploits that might adorn a tale of romance, the young prince recalled his people from the distant quarters to which they had been driven, organized them into a regular military body, drove the oppressors from post after post, and finally became undisputed ruler of Coorg, expelling the Mahommedan settlers who had been forcibly introduced, as above described. Thus, Veer Rajunder sustained a successful contest against his mighty neighbour, in whose eye Coorg had acquired great importance, as a decisive struggle with the rising power of the East India Company was impending, when the possession of Coorg by the enemy might seal the fate of Seringapatam. The Company's Government, on the other hand, was equally aware of the stratagetic value of Coorg; while Veer Rajunder dreaded and hated Tippoo, from whom he could expect no mercy, and whose assurances and promises he could never trust. All his hopes, therefore, depended on his success in gaining the support of a powerful ally, and his eyes were naturally directed towards the rising star of the Company. The union of Tippoo's enemies was effected without difficulty. Mutta Bhatta, an agent of Veer Rajunder, arrived at Tellicherry, ostensibly for the

[1] A British fugitive, who had also been lucky enough to effect his escape, saw this Rajah, in 1793, at his residence at Nocknab, and describes him as a young man buckishly dressed in nankeen pantaloons, European boots, and a shirt made in the English fashion.

purpose of purchasing a horse and other articles, but really for that of having an interview with the Company's representative. This he effected, and carried a letter back to Coorg, containing a proposal for a cordial alliance. The Rajah cheerfully consented. He agreed to procure draught cattle for the Bombay army, and immediately commenced forays into the Mysore, Tippoo's cattle being superior to those of Coorg. In a short time he despatched upwards of 500 head to Tellicherry; and shortly after this proof of his sincerity, the Company concluded with him the following agreement:—

Articles of Agreement entered into between Robert Taylor, Chief, and Factors at Tellicherry, in behalf of the Honourable United East India Company, on the one part, and Alery Vera, Rajah of Coorg, on the other part.

1st. A firm and perpetual friendship shall subsist between both parties, as long as the Sun and Moon shall endure.

2nd. Tippoo Sultan and his adherents shall be considered as the common enemy of both parties, and in the prosecution of the war, in which the English are at present engaged, the Coorg Rajah shall, whenever it may be in his power, do his utmost to distress the enemy, and admit the English troops at any time to pass through his dominions, should they have occasion to penetrate the enemy's country from this (the Malabar) coast. He, moreover, engages to furnish them with such supplies of provisions as his country can afford, at reasonable rates, and to join the English army with such a force as he can spare, whenever any operations are carried on above the Ghauts (mountains), or in the country of Tippoo Sultan.

3rd. The Rajah engages to give the Company the preference in purchasing at a reasonable and moderate price such articles of commerce as are produced in his country, and the Company may want, and he engages not to permit any other European nation to interfere in this respect.

4th. The English East India Company engages to do everything in their power to render him, the Coorg Rajah, independent of Tippoo, in the same manner as the other powers who have entered into an alliance with the Company; and they shall, whenever a peace takes place, insist upon it as an express stipulation, that the Coorg Rajah shall be considered as the friend and ally of the Honourable Company, and in no manner subject to the control or authority of Tippoo, of whom he shall be declared totally independent.

5th. Should the Rajah's family, or that of any of his subjects, have occasion, in the present troubles, to take refuge at Tellicherry, the Company engages to receive them at the foot of the Ghauts, and conduct them in safety to Tellicherry under a guard of Sepoys, where they shall find an asylum and be protected during the troubles; a house shall be provided for them during their residence at Tellicherry, and the families shall be returned in safety whenever required. In testimony of the perpetual friendship that shall subsist between both parties, which neither party will ever disturb, we jointly call God, the Sun, the Moon, and the World, to witness this our agreement and mutual pledge of faith.

Concluded at Tellicherry, this 26th day of October, in the year of the Christian Era 1790.

By Robert Taylor, Chief, and Factors, in the names of the English East India Company, the Governor-General of Bengal, and the Governor of Bombay, on the one part, and by Alery Vera, Rajah, on the other, each of the parties present, that is to say, the Chief and Factors of Tellicherry, and Alery Vera, Rajah of Coorg, having hereunto put their names and seals at Tellicherry, the day and year above written, and mutually exchanged copies of this Agreement.

(Signed) ROBERT TAYLOR.
" LAWRENCE SHAW. (Seal.)
" SAMUEL INCE.
The Seal of the Rajah. (Seal.)

It will be seen that by the second clause of the above Treaty, the Rajah agreed to permit the British troops to pass through "his dominions, and penetrate into the enemy's country from this (the Malabar) coast." The Bombay army, under the command of General Abercromby, having by this means a road opened to Mysore, was enabled to land, advance, and ascend the Ghauts, by the Heggala Pass, through Coorg, and form a conjunction with the army of Lord Cornwallis, who, thus timely and powerfully reinforced, defeated Tippoo, and dictated a peace under the walls of Seringapatam, by which the Sultan ceded half his dominions to the Company.

The Rajah, indeed, although unable, like the Nizam, to bring to our assistance, crowds of troops, or such effective aid as the Mahrattas, yet, by receiving the British as a friendly power, by collecting and furnishing, at his own cost, the indispensable supplies of grain and cattle for their subsistence, and by leading his own troops and fighting at their head, on the side of the British, faithfully and to the utmost of his power, performed his part of the Treaty, and did all to promote the views and interests of the Company, notwithstanding the repeated endeavours of Tippoo to gain him over. Upon one occasion, the latter condescended so far as to send a confidential officer, Kadar Khan Kesagi, a friend of Veer Rajunder, with an autograph of Tippoo, and letters from Mir Saduk, the Prime Minister, and Purnayah, the Minister of Finance, soliciting Veer Rajunder's forgiveness and friendship. Veer Rajunder showed these letters to Sir Robert Abercromby, and replied to Tippoo: "By similar fair speeches and promises, you have formerly deceived and ruined Coorg. God has given me one tongue, with which I have pledged fidelity to the Company. I have not two tongues, like you."

It would have been impossible for so brave a man not to have appreciated valour in others. Accordingly, we find that, after the battle which terminated so disastrously for Tippoo Sultan, the Rajah expressed his admiration and delight at

British courage, by passing along the lines, addressing the European soldiers, and enthusiastically exclaiming, that heroes like the English ought to be carried in palanquins, and not be made to march to the field of battle. How greatly his services were appreciated will appear from the following :—

Declaration made by Lieut.-General Sir Robert Abercromby, Commander-in-Chief of the Bombay Army in the War against Tippoo Sultan, dated Cannanore, 31st March, 1793.

Hallaree Veera Rajah, Rajah of Coorg, being desirous that the situation in which he stands with regard to the Honourable English East India Company may be clearly understood by all their servants, I hereby declare and certify—

1st. That the said Rajah at the commencement of the late war with Tippoo Sultan (*the Rajah being then in possession of the greater part of the Coorg country, the remainder of which he afterwards recovered without the aid of the Company*), offered his assistance to the Honourable Company, which was accepted, and an agreement was accordingly entered into between him on his own behalf, and Robert Taylor, Esq., Chief of Tellicherry, on the part of the Company, as will appear by the records of that settlement.

2nd. That the Rajah entered most heartily into the war, and supplied the Bombay army under my command with a quantity of grain and cattle, without which the troops would have been greatly distressed, and for which the Rajah has hitherto declined taking any pecuniary compensation.

3rd. That from the commencement of the war till its conclusion, the Rajah continued most firmly attached to the interests of the Company, notwithstanding the repeated attempts of Tippoo to seduce him.

4th. That in March last, on settling the articles of the Treaty of Peace, at Seringapatam, Lord Cornwallis, in consideration of the noble and disinterested conduct of the Rajah, determined to render him entirely independent of Tippoo, and to extend to him and his country the protection of the Company. The numberless objections that were made to this were overruled, and the tribute amounting to eight thousand (8000) Hoons, *said to have been annually paid* to Tippoo from the Coorg country, was transferred to the Company.

5th. That the Rajah readily agrees to pay the Company annually (8000) Hoons for their friendship and protection, *though he declares that Tippoo never received that sum from his country.*

6th. That no interference was ever intended on the part of the Company in the interior management of the Rajah's country, trusting that a Prince possessing the most liberal sentiments will make the happiness of his people his constant study.

Given under my hand and seal at Cannanore, this day, the thirty-first of March, in the year of our Lord, one thousand seven hundred and ninety-three.

[Seal] (Signed) Robert Abercromby,
Lieut.-General.

N.B.—The Hoons are reckoned at three rupees each; the sum, therefore, that the Rajah will have to pay annually at Tellicherry, amounts to twenty-four thousand rupees.

(Signed) Robert Abercromby, Lieut.-General.

Great in every respect as Lord Cornwallis was, he was greatest in his sense of justice. He had chastised and humbled Tippoo, not for any attack on British power, but for a wanton outrage on a British ally; and when he deprived Tippoo of half his dominions, and forced him to pay three crores of rupees, he partitioned the former fairly among the allies, whose valour had aided the English, not forgetting the Rajah of Coorg.

In the preliminaries of peace, no express provision had been made for the Rajah's protection; but in the draught of the definitive Treaty, Tippoo was made to resign all pretensions to

Coorg. For this provision in his favour, the Rajah was principally indebted to Sir Robert Abercromby. As the besiegers drew off their artillery and prepared for their departure for their respective countries, Sir Robert Abercromby and Col. James Hartley went to the Governor-General, and during a visit of three days, interposed their good offices in behalf of the Coorg ally. "We," said Sir Robert, "are retiring from Bombay with our army. The Rajah of Coorg—our faithful ally from the commencement of the war, who has served us at all times to the utmost of his power, opened his country to our troops, supplied us with provisions during the whole course of hostilities, and risked his life in many a fight against Tippoo, and to whom we have given the most solemn assurances of friendship and protection—will now be left to the mercy of his still too powerful neighbour and dreadful enemy." This remonstrance had, as has been seen, the desired effect; and lucky was it for the Rajah that it had, for Tippoo had, no doubt, destined him for a conspicuous example of the direful consequences of renouncing his allegiance.[1] It must be confessed that Tippoo Sultan had just reason for complaint; the territory of the Rajah commanded the best approach to his capital, from the sea; and he insisted that to demand a territory which abutted on his very capital, and was not contiguous to the country of any of the allies, was a real infringement of the preliminary articles. No sooner, therefore, did he see the condition in favour of Veer Rajunder, than he burst into a paroxysm of fury that approached to absolute frenzy. "To which of their territories," said he, "is Coorg adjacent? Why do they not ask at once for Seringapatam? They know

[1] Some idea of the fate which awaited Veer Rajunder, had he fallen into Tippoo's hands, may be formed from what befel seventeen British officers, and General Matthews, who were all taken prisoners by him: the former were compelled to swallow the infused juice of the milky-hedge-tree, and all miserably perished in the prisons of Kavel Droog and Seringapatam. The General himself did not expire by poison; but, horrid to relate, had his head wrung from his body by the tiger fangs of the Jetties, a set of slaves trained up to gratify their master with this infernal piece of dexterity.

that I would sooner have died in the breach than have consented to such a cession, and durst not bring it forward till they had treacherously obtained my children and my treasure." He refused, in consequence, to sign the treaty solely on this ground, nor was it until Lord Cornwallis had repointed his guns against Seringapatam, that Tippoo's hostage sons presented the document fully ratified to Lord Cornwallis.

Peace being concluded, Veer Rajunder was required to give back the districts which he had lately wrested from the Sultan, and informed that he was expected in future to pay his tribute to the English Government. He was indignant at both these propositions, for he had expected some better reward for his important services. Sir Robert Abercromby did all in his power to pacify the brave ally, who had served him so well; but, of course, the Mysore territory had to be restored, and the dream of an "independent principality of Coorg" could not be realized. Sir Robert humoured, however, Veer Rajunder, by the drawing up of a document, at his last meeting with the Rajah, in March, 1793. In this paper, the Rajah was permitted to assert, that he had been an independent Prince, and had never paid tribute to Mysore, while, at the same time, he declared his willingness "to pay, of his own free will, the sum of 800 pagodas to the Company every year, for their friendship and protection." The Company, on the other hand, engaged to give no molestation to the Rajah, and in no wise to interfere with the Government of Coorg, as the Rajah was quite competent to take care of his own affairs.

From this time to the end of his life, Veer Rajunder remained the trusty friend of the Company, and his affairs prospered. In 1795, he communicated to the English Government, the intelligence he had obtained, through some spies, that Tippoo Sultan was concerting plans with the Mahrattas; and in the beginning of 1799, we find him again actively employed in assisting the Bombay troops, marching towards Seringapatam, with Coolies, draught cattle and elephants, grain, and sheep. The Rajah was present at the battle of Sedaseer, of which he gave the following accurate and animated description in a letter addressed to the Governor-General, who received it on the 12th of April, 1799.

"On Tuesday, Mag Bohd Amawasy, in the year Ka Gust, about forty-one days ago, myself, Captain Mahoney, and some other English Sirdars, went to the hill of Sedaseer, which is within my territories. This mountain, which is exceedingly lofty, the English Sirdars and myself ascended, and we remained there. Having from thence reconnoitred, we observed nothing for the first four or five hours (Malabar hours); after this we observed one large tent in the direction of Periapatam, which is within the territories of Tippoo Sultan, and continued to see some other white tents rising; a large green tent then appeared, and then another tent, which was red, and after that five or six hundred tents. Upon this, the English Sirdars and myself were satisfied that it was the army of Tippoo Sultan; we then returned to the English army at Sadapoor, and acquainted the General that Tippoo's army was at Periapatam. The army was accordingly prepared, as were also the two battalions at Sedaseer, under the command of Colonel Montresor. The enemy being apprised of the English post at Sedaseer, and that it would therefore be impossible to advance by the Sedapoor road, were advancing by the high road of Balala, through the talook of Kigalnaad, three coss to the right of Sedapoor, the same road by which Hyder Naik formerly invaded the Coorg country. Upon receiving a report that they were approaching by the Balala road, and were near to Veer Rajah-indra-pellak, we all considered and determined that four or five thousand Coorgs should be stationed on that road. They were accordingly posted there, with orders to cut off Tippoo if he should advance. About one hundred or one hundred and fifty Coorgs were attached to myself: arrangements were also made in the different paths which communicated between the two frontiers. Things being in this state, we again reconnoitred from the hill of Sedaseer, and General Hartley went in the morning to Sedapoor. On the same day Tippoo, with his whole force, began his march by the Sedaseer road. General Hartley was prepared at this time. Tippoo's army advanced close to the two battalions under the command of Colonel Montresor, and there was a severe action. After the battle commenced, the two battalions killed a great many of Tippoo's people. Tippoo, unable to sustain the fire of the battalions, and having no road by which to advance, divided his army into five divisions, with the intention of getting into the rear of Colonel Montresor's battalions, by a secret path. The Colonel, having received intelligence of this division, made a disposition of his forces so as to sustain both attacks, and maintained the fight until the morning, uninterruptedly, till two o'clock. The enemy were beaten and unable to show their faces. When this information reached the main body, General Stuart, in order to assist the force at Sedapoor, marched with two regiments of Europeans, keeping the remainder of the army in the plain of Karrydygood. Upon this occasion I accompanied General Stuart. Tippoo, in order to prevent the two regiments from advancing to the relief of the troops of Sadaseer, was posted on the road between. General Stuart, upon approaching, ordered the two regiments to attack the enemy. A severe action then ensued, in which I was present. To describe the battle which General Stuart fought with these two regiments of Europeans, the discipline, valour, strength, and magnanimity of the troops, the courageous attack upon the army of Tippoo, surpasses all example in this world. In our Shasters and Purranas, the battles fought by Allered and Maharul have been much celebrated, but they are unequal to this battle; it exceeds my ability to describe this action, at length, to your Lordship. In this manner Tippoo's army was beaten. The action with the two regiments lasted about three hours and a half. A Sirdar of high rank with Tippoo, the Benky Nabob, fell in this action; the first and second buckshies of a body of 6000 men, being wounded with musket balls, were taken prisoners. I have also heard that five or six other officers of rank with the enemy have fallen; many of the enemy were slain, and many wounded; the remainder having thrown away their muskets, swords, and turbans, and thinking it sufficient to save their lives, fled in the greatest confusion. Tippoo having collected the remains of his troops, returned to Periapatam.

"Veer Rajunder Wadeer."

To this gallant resistance of the advanced brigade at Sadaseer, the British army stood indebted, not only for its subsequent conquest of the Mysore, but for its very existence in that country as an offensive power. Had the advanced posts been carried, the whole of the Bombay force must have been driven back, and its junction with that under General Harris either totally prevented, or rendered ineffective; while the boast and triumph of Tippoo could not have failed to have allured to his standard the inhabitants of Malabar, then ripe for revolt; and thus, in proportion as the resources of the Sultan would have been increased, those of the British would have been diminished.

While Seringapatam was being besieged, the Rajah also despatched an expedition of Coorgs, under Subaya and Bopu, into the Tolu country, the greater part of which was wrested from the Mussulmans, and plundered in Coorg style. His services, indeed, were considered so important, that the Earl of Mornington, Governor-General of India, bore his testimony to them in two official despatches, addressed to different officers of his Majesty's Government. The portion of the first of these two letters which refers to the Rajah, is as follows:—

The Earl of Mornington, Governor-General of India, to the Commissioners of Malabar.

Fort St. George, 10th April, 1799.

GENTLEMEN,—* * * The Rajah of Coorg has seconded my views and the exertion of the Company's servants on this occasion with a degree of spirit, energy, and fidelity which confirms the high character he had justly obtained in the late war. I have expressed my sense of his zealous attachment and honourable services in a letter to him, which will be forwarded to you by the Persian translator, with a copy for your information. I think it proper to apprise you that I have determined, as a testimony of the satisfaction which his conduct has afforded me, and with a view of encouraging the imitation of his example among other tributaries of the Company, to relinquish the tribute at present payable by the Rajah, and to substitute some annual acknowledgment of the Company's claim on his allegiance. The Government of Bombay will receive the necessary directions from me for giving effect to this arrangement. I have no doubt that the exertions of the Rajah, to collect grain for the use of the army, will be continued so long as they shall be necessary, with the same spirit that has hitherto distinguished them, and I am equally confident that those exertions will be ably and zealously seconded by you, and by those under your orders on the coast of Malabar.

* * * I entirely agree with you in your construction of the letter from Ayappin to the Rajah of Coorg, a copy of which was enclosed in your despatch of the 25th March; and I desire you will signify to the Rajah, that I have viewed with the utmost contempt and indignation this weak and insidious attempt of Tippoo Sultan to cast doubts upon the faith of an ally whose attachment, fortitude, wisdom, and integrity, have secured the affection and admiration of the British Government. * * * *

I am, Gentlemen, &c.

(Signed) MORNINGTON.

The portion of the other letter, referring to the same, is as follows:—

The Earl of Mornington to the Honourable Jonathan Duncan, Governor of Bombay.

Fort St. George, 8th May, 1799.

SIR,—The exemplary conduct and distinguished character of the Coorg Rajah, having rendered me desirous of manifesting some public testimony of my approbation of his recent services, the remission of his annual tribute to the Company appears to me to be a measure which would combine the effects of an honourable distinction and a profitable reward. My intention is, that of the whole amount of the Rajah's present tribute, which I understand to be about 24,000 rupees, a sum not exceeding 1000 rupees be reserved to the Company, or that, in place of tribute, some article of considerable value be annually required from him as an acknowledgment of his allegiance to the British Government. I request that, after having determined the nature of the acknowledgment to be required according to your judgment, you will take the necessary measures for carrying my intention into effect. I think the arrangement should be made to take place from the day of the junction of the army of Bombay with the detachment commanded by Major-General Flood.

I am, &c. &c.

(Signed) MORNINGTON.

In addition to these testimonials, the Marquis Wellesley, Governor-General, sent him, on the 23rd of May, a handsome sword, accompanied with a letter of thanks; General Harris presented him with one of Tippoo's chargers, one of his palkees (palanquins), and one of his howdas; and the East India Company commuted the money payment of the tribute into the gift of an elephant, to be presented to them annually. The Governor-General's letter was as follows:—

To the Rajah of Coorg. 23rd May, 1804.

I have had frequent occasion to express to you the sentiments of approbation with which I have contemplated the zeal and attachment which you have uniformly manifested during a long course of years towards the British Government; I have been apprised of the views and wishes which you entertain with respect to an extension of your territory. The necessity of a previous investigation of the means of framing an arrangement for that purpose has occasioned some delay.

Being fully impressed with a sense of your merits as a faithful friend and adherent of the British Government, and being anxious to afford you a proof of the sentiments of regard and respect which I entertain for your character, I have directed Captain Mahoney, who formerly resided with you on the part of the British Government, to proceed to your court for the purpose of carrying into effect the arrangements which I have adopted for an extension of your territory. I refer you for information respecting the details of this arrangement to Captain Mahoney, who will attend you for that purpose, and will have the pleasure of delivering this letter.

As an additional mark of my personal regard and esteem, I request your acceptance of a sword, which will be transmitted to Captain Mahoney with the utmost practicable expedition, for the purpose of being presented to you in my name.

(Signed) WELLESLEY.

The Marquis's illustrious brother, the Duke of Wellington, at that time Colonel Wellesley, had also, in the previous year, borne his testimony to the Rajah's services.[1] In a letter to Lord Clive, and dated Seringapatam, Jan. 1st, 1803, after saying that no part of the Mysore territory can be given to Veray, for political reasons connected with the relations of

[1] *Despatches*, vol. i. p. 32.

the recently established Government of Mysore to the Government of the Company, he thus proceeds:—

"The services of the Rajah of Coorg, however, still deserve remuneration. It appears by Captain Mahoney's accounts, that he expended sums of money, and furnished supplies of cattle and provisions, in the late war against Tippoo Sultan, of a value amounting to about four lacs of rupees. If he had consented to be reimbursed this expenditure, he would have received bonds of the Bombay Government for this sum of money, bearing interest at 12 per cent. per annum, in the beginning of the year 1799, and in this manner would have added two lacs of rupees to the sum above mentioned. It may, therefore, be fairly concluded, that, by the liberality of the Rajah, the Company's treasury is richer at this moment, by not less than six lacs of rupees, than it would have been if he had taken payment of the money expended, and for the supplies furnished by him. In this view of the question, I do not take into consideration the nature of his services, or the time at which they were rendered; but I have stated, particularly, what the supplies furnished by him would have cost the Company if they had been furnished by any other person, as I found thereon the amount of the remuneration which I intend to recommend your Lordship to grant him."

Veer Rajunder was now left in the free and full possession of his principality, and lived on the most friendly terms with the Mysore Residents, the Madras Governor, Sir George Barlow, Lord W. Bentinck, and the Governor-General, the Marquis of Wellesley. About the time his first grandson was born to him, he was passionately attached to his new wife, the Ranee Mahadeva, who had borne him two daughters, and he might have lived and died a happy man if he had had a son and heir, had not mistrusted his nearest relatives, and if his violent temper had not often carried him beyond the bounds of humanity. He lived in constant dread of poison;

and it is highly probable that the frenzy which appeared at times to seize him, and during which he committed acts he sincerely regretted when he recovered his reason, was caused by drugs administered to him in spite of all his caution. In 1807 he caused a history of his house to be written, a work which, together with its translation, by Mr. Robert Abercromby, is now in course of publication, by the orders and at the expense of the Government of Madras.

The concluding lines of this Rajendraname, or history, afford a glimpse of the alternations of hope and fear which agitated his heart. He thus expresses himself:—"On the 7th of the Pushya month, Ractaxi year (1805), Captain Mahoney brought the sword, sent by Marquis Wellesley from Bengal, and fastened it round the Rajah's waist. In the Magha month (Feb. 7, 1806), Veer Rajunder told Captain Mahoney, for the information of the Governor-General, that on the day of his second marriage, when he sat on the throne with his Ranee, he had determined, that any son of his by this wife should be his successor; that his wife had borne him two daughters. If any son be hereafter born of her, he would be the heir; but if it was the will of God that she should bear no son, then the three sons of his concubine, called Rajashekerappa, Shishushekappa, and Chandrashekarappa, should succeed to the throne. Since the above date, two more daughters, in all four, have been borne by the Ranee Mahadeva, who died at three o'clock, on Sunday, the 7th of the month Jashta, 4909 Prabhava year. As, by her death, the Rajah's hopes of having a son by her were blasted, and he was afraid, lest, if the succession devolved on the sons of another mother, they would create trouble to the four daughters of his lawful Queen, the Rajah determined that of the four daughters the eldest should be married, and whatever son she might have, he should be named Veer Rajunder, receive the Rajah's seal, and the sword which was presented to him by Marquis Wellesley, and be the successor to the throne. If she should, however, have no son, the son of either of her younger sisters, according to seniority, should be the successor, and so long as the line of any of his four above-mentioned daughters continued, none of the heirs of the other mother should succeed to the throne; but, upon the family of his four daughters being extinct, the fittest of the above three sons, or their posterity, should succeed. The Rajah, sensible of the instability of human life, and all other things, has thought proper now to determine and record this matter, in order that no wrong may hereafter occur; and he requests that the English Sarkar will be the guardian of his family, and see the execution of the above-written will attended to.

"In order that the Rajah's heirs may be acquainted with his resolution, he has written a copy thereof, to which he has affixed his seal and signature, and which is lodged in the palace treasury."

We quote the above passage because it proves the Rajah's fondness for the four daughters of his beloved Ranee; his morbid anxiety for being succeeded by a grandson, at least, of his own name; his fears regarding the safety of his beloved daughter, in case of one of his other relatives (brothers) succeeding him, and his absolute confidence in the English Sarkar.

Great as was the state of mental excitement under which the Rajah had been for some time suffering, it was still further increased by the death, in May, 1807, of his beloved Ranee Mahadeva, and, as he suspected she had been destroyed by sorceries, he dreaded a similar fate. Nor was this all: a conspiracy, in which the whole of his Coorg guards were implicated, broke out, and was only suppressed by the massacre, in the palace yard, of 300 Coorgs by the African troops in the pay of the Rajah. Veer Rajunder is said to have himself shot twenty-five of the insurgents from a balcony window.

A gloomy melancholy appears to have taken possession of him from that moment; the only object for which he cared to live being to obtain the sanction of the Supreme Government for his settlement of the succession upon which he thought the future happiness, if not the very safety, of his beloved daughter and her sisters depended; and, although his requests were never distinctly granted, he believed they were. The nearer his end approached the more suspicious he became. Mistrusting his two brothers, Appajii and Ling Rajunder, he one morning despatched executioners to bring him their heads, and, although he afterwards relented, his repentance came too late to save the life of Appajii. Ling Rajunder escaped. On another occasion, he ordered four of his principal officers to be put to death, and was overwhelmed with horror and remorse when, on calling for them after his frenzy had abated, he was informed that they had been executed in obedience to his command. Fearing that these deeds might be reported to the Supreme Government, and dreading their displeasure, he twice attempted his own life, once with a razor, and once by swallowing poison; but, on both occasions, was recovered by Dr. Ingledew. The Supreme Government, in answer to the reports sent to them, pitied, pardoned, and comforted, by kind assurances, the poor distracted Rajah. All was of no avail. When the gloom of the monsoon of 1809 set in, he sank by degrees. Upon his violence diminishing, he felt more kindly towards his son-in-law, and appointed him Dewan during Dewa Ammajee's minority. His mind now fully recovered its tone: on the 9th of June he sent for his favourite daughter, gave his seal into her hand, and expired. He lies buried in one of the mausoleums which grace the hill overlooking the town of Mercara.

Thus died Veer Rajunder Wadeer, Rajah of Coorg, one of the few Indians on whom Mill pronounces a eulogium:—

"The circumstances in which he (the Rajah) had been placed by misfortune, broke many of the fetters which bind the understandings of his countrymen; and he manifested an enlargement of mind seldom witnessed amongst those matchless slaves of prejudice. Not only had trials invigorated his faculties, but he displayed a generosity and a heroism worthy of a much more civilized state of society. Bred in adversity, and obliged to submit to the duties of a religion which was foreign to his caste, the Rajah's mind was indeed enlarged beyond the prejudices which generally fetter the natives in India: he was desirous of seeing, and being instructed; went on board the ships at Tellicherry; was fond of conversing with our officers; of making himself acquainted with our discipline; and on many occasions, particularly on horseback, adopted the English dress." But the Rajah's character will be better understood from the following circumstances.

At the time that the Bombay army was first ascending the Ghauts, the Rajah, after clearing the greater part of his country of the enemy, was employed in the blockade of Mercara, which Tippoo had fortified with cannon, and maintained as a post in the heart of his country. A detachment sent from Seringapatam to relieve it was surrounded, and summoned to lay down their arms. The officer who commanded this corps having been friendly to the Rajah, and particularly instrumental in assisting him to escape from Tippoo's power, made himself known; and having represented to him that he should not only be dismissed from the Sultan's service if he did not execute his orders, but that his master's vengeance would be wreaked upon his innocent family, the Rajah allowed him both to send in his provisions, and to return safe with his detachment.

Fearful what appearance this transaction might have to his friends the English, the Rajah explained the whole matter in a letter to General Abercromby, and said that his allowing the provisions to be thrown into the place was of no consequence, and would not protract the siege a few weeks.

The General, fully convinced of the Rajah's sincerity, and struck with his conduct, offered to send a detachment to assist him in recovering Mercara from the enemy. This, with many expressions of gratitude, he declined; saying, he should in time be able to effect the object himself, and was determined to regain his capital with his own troops.

The Rajah's generosity to his friend in the Sultan's service, and his magnanimity in prosecuting the siege with his own people, were soon rewarded by the surrender of his capital, which, with the spirit of a Spartan, he dismantled of its defences—resolved to leave no harbour for his enemies, and that his Coorgs should depend solely on their own bravery for the defence of their country.

We have seen that, when dying, Veer Rajunder placed his seal in the hands of his daughter Dewa Ammajee, which was equivalent to the declaring her his successor; and accordingly she became, on the death of her father, Ranee of Coorg, and was acknowledged as such in a letter of the Marquis of Hastings, dated April, 2, 1809. She did not, however, retain the dignity long, for Ling Rajunder Wadeer, the brother of the deceased Rajah, made himself Regent of Coorg, and guardian of his niece, before the end of 1810. In 1811 he announced to the Government of Fort St. George that he had assumed the Government of Coorg in his own name. Mr. Cole, the Resident of Mysore, was ordered to make inquiry in Coorg, as to the lawfulness of Ling Rajunder's claim to the throne. The inquiry was not made, but the Resident's own individual opinion was, that female succession in Coorg was contrary to the Shasters, or laws. The Supreme Government, in the mean time, put off the decision of the somewhat intricate question until the Ranee should attain her majority, when she might prove her claims; and no protest was made against Ling Rajunder's assumption of power. Before the end of 1812, Ling Rajunder had firmly established himself; fearing, however, some change in the measures of the Supreme Government, he prevented, as far as lay in his power, all communication between Coorg and the surrounding territory of the Company. The frontiers were guarded, and nobody was allowed to pass out or in without the Rajah's permission. European visitors were treated with profuse hospitality, and overwhelmed with civilities, but all communication between them and the natives of the country was carefully prevented. Ling Rajunder died in 1820, at the age of 45, after having held possession of Coorg for eleven years. His elder brother, Veer Rajunder, had died at about the same time of life. Like him, he suspected that he died a victim to magic arts, employed by enemies among his own people. No doubt many hated him in secret; and it is not unlikely that poison may have been administered to him, for poison was as freely used in Coorg as sorcery. This prince has been accused of having committed many cruelties and much oppression; but there does not appear to be sufficient evidence forthcoming to substantiate the charge. His widow, inconsolable for the death of her husband, committed suicide by swallowing diamond dust, the custom of Suttee not being known in Coorg. She was buried in the same tomb with her husband.

General Welsh, in his *Military Reminiscences,* gives the following amusing account of a visit which he paid Ling Rajunder in the year 1811:—

"On the 19th of March, 1811, having heard much in praise of the sport in Coorg, and being at leisure for such a trip, I set out from Bangalore, having a letter of introduction from the Honourable Arthur Cole, Resident at Mysore, and in company with Lieutenant W. Williamson, a young man of my own corps, both a keen and hardy sportsman as well as a very agreeable companion. We travelled post, in palanquin, to Verajenderpett, a distance of 150 miles. On the 22nd of March, after a hearty breakfast, provided for us by the Rajah's people gratis, we mounted two large elephants at daybreak, and proceeded over hills and through vales, up and down, zigzag, now at the bottom of deep ravines, then at the top of precipices, till at last, after eight hours' fagging, we reached the palace, built for the accommodation of Europeans, outside the stone fort of Mercara, the capital. The place is delightfully situated on an eminence near the summit of a range of lofty and difficult mountains. The pass up these mountains being fortified and defended, however, would make it a very strong place, for it completely commands every approach on the other side. The distance we estimated at twenty-four miles. The Rajah's own palace is inside the fort; but his horse and elephant stables are outside, on the slope of the glacis. The town is remarkably clean and well built; about half a mile off, by an excellent high road, and at the further extremity, is a rising ground, with a strong mud barrier, after entering which you come upon a small plain, with a magnificent tomb, erected by the present Rajah to the memory of his late brother and wife. It is much in the style of Mahommedan edifices, being a wide square, with a handsome dome in the centre, and four turrets at the angles. On the top of the dome is a gold ball, with a weathercock above it, and all the window-bars are made of solid brass.

"On this spot we met, by appointment, Maha Swami, at half-past three in the evening. He was dressed in a major-general's uniform, appeared to be about thirty years of age, with very handsome features, and a person in which were joined both activity and strength. He immediately shook hands with us, and desired us to be seated, after a short conversation in Hindustani, which he at first addressed to an interpreter, until he found that I could speak and understand him in that language. He then produced several rifles, ready loaded, ordered cocoa-nuts to be hoisted on the tops of spears fifty yards off, and then desired us to fire. Suffice it to say, he beat us both most completely, splitting every nut he fired at in the centre, while we either struck the sides or missed entirely. After this, he asked us to take a ride with him; a beautiful English horse was brought to me, an Arabian to Lieut. Williamson, and he himself also rode a very fine Arabian. We rattled about in the square for half an hour, when he desired us to alight and rest ourselves, and, taking a long spear, performed several feats with it, still on horseback, with great grace and dexterity. Our horses being again brought, we remounted, and proceeded with him to the fort, the Rajah insisting on our riding one on each side of him all the way. On entering his palace, we were amused by a set of dancing girls, keeping time to reels and country dances, played on two fiddles; and the Maha Swami showed us various portraits of himself, the Prince of Wales, General Wellesley, &c. He then took us into another apartment, and exhibited to us a dozen of highly finished single and double rifles, by Manton and Gover, fowling-pieces, pistols, &c.; then an air-gun, which he desired us to try. It was now seven P.M., and torchlight had succeeded the daylight in his court-yard; we took aim out of the window at various things, and hit them, and I even knocked down a lime, a species of small lemon, off the top of a cocoa-nut, so uncommonly true did it carry. His son and several relatives were next introduced to us, all fine-looking boys; and the heir apparent, being about seven or eight years old, dressed in a general's uniform, with a sword by his side, put me in mind of some old French prints, in which the girls are dressed in hoops and farthingales, and the boys with bag-wigs and small swords. Ram-fights, &c. were going on all this time in the yard, as it were to amuse the attendants, and two of the rams had four horns each; then a lion made his appearance, led by a dozen men with a strong rope. He appeared very tame, played with his leaders, and suffered me to go up to him and pat him on the back. Next came a large royal tiger and two panthers, the former having his claws pared, but very savage, trying every instant to break loose. We took leave at half-past seven, quite pleased with the kind and affable treatment of this prince, who, I am inclined to believe, is adored by his people.

"I must now describe our own habitation, built on a small island, surrounded by paddy ground, now dry, for the sole accommodation of Europeans. It is a large square, having a hall in the centre, a large covered-in veranda all round it, and four bedrooms projecting at the angles of the veranda, all on the upper story, the lower rooms serving for the guard, attendants, store-rooms, &c. It stands on a square of seventy feet, the veranda having thirty-eight glass windows, with Venetian blinds outside. The bedrooms have sixteen windows, and the hall eight glass doors, every part being neatly furnished in the English style, with beds, tables, card-tables, writing-boxes, chairs, chandeliers, settees, &c. &c.; and there is an old butler, of my early Velore friend, Colonel Ridgway Mealay, and a dozen active servants, who very speedily produced an English breakfast or dinner, served up on handsome Queen's ware, with every kind of European liquor; and, what is still more extraordinary, the cook bakes good bread.

"After all our exertions of this day, it may readily be supposed we slept soundly, and on the morning of the 23rd, rose betimes, as usual—a custom which I most strenuously recommend to all young men doomed to spend their time in the East—and went to visit the Rajah's stud and elephants; and amongst the latter found a young white one, about two years old, most perfectly formed, with flaxen hair, light eyes, and fair skin. Of these animals, as his country abounds in them, he has great abundance. After breakfast, we were astonished by a visit from the Maha Swami, in state. No longer disguised in a European dress, he appeared in his native robes, richly decorated with jewels; and, in my eyes, he appeared a much handsomer man. He sat a few minutes, and then told us that he had received intelligence of a wild elephant, and would, if we pleased, accompany us to go and shoot him. To us this was the most acceptable offer he could have made. We retired to prepare ourselves and our shooting apparatus, and on our return from our own rooms, found his Highness ready with elephants and attendants. Away we set, the Rajah himself driving the one I rode, sitting across its neck, with a hook in his right hand and a knife in the other, to cut down any small branches of trees likely to incommode me in the excursion. Such a man, thought I, at the head of his followers, must be invincible—so perfectly different from the effeminate grandeur of most Eastern potentates. Arrived at the spot, which was only about a mile off, we dismounted; and, while the people were preparing seats on trees for our reception, amused ourselves shooting arrows at a mark, in which, as usual, the Rajah beat us hollow. When all was ready, each climbed his own tree, the Rajah between us, and sat in a snug little wicker box, with three guns of the Rajah's each, and two of his eunuchs to load our pieces. The Rajah had a single rifle, carrying a twelve-ounce ball, and two double ones of one ounce each. Upon the animal's approach, we made a general discharge at him; the creature rolled over instantaneously, carrying away several small trees, as he extended his enormous bulk upon the ground. It stood ten feet high, and was in excellent condition; the tusks were two feet outside, and nearly three feet long, when extracted, and the length of the body was nearly the same as its height. . . . Here, supposing our day's work was concluded, we prepared to take leave, but we were yet to learn something further of the kind attentions of this excellent prince. He told us, that having kept us so long from our own tiffin (luncheon), it being then three o'clock, he had ordered a dinner to be brought out for us; and, to our surprise, we found a house built of leaves, a table and chairs, a dinner, consisting of pillawe, mutton cutlets, curry, &c., all ready for us. Nor was this all; the Rajah followed us in, and begged us to excuse him, as he was not very well, but left his servants with guns, powder, shot, &c., and four elephants, desiring us to amuse ourselves after dinner as we pleased. We accordingly dined, and then beat a thick jungle for game, though without success, it being the dry season, when they retire into the most inaccessible parts of the mountains. At five P.M. we returned to our palace, well satisfied with the adventures of the day.

"On the 25th of March, we paid our parting visit to the Maha Swami, and received from him the following presents—two gold-handled Coorg knives, two panther-skin caps, two sandal-wood sticks, one royal tiger and two panther skins; and parted from him with mutual expressions of esteem and regard."

The present ex-Rajah, named after his illustrious uncle, Veer Rajunder Wadeer, succeeded, and was acknowledged without difficulty by the British Government, which appears to have desisted from any further investigation of the succession question, and to have entirely passed over the claims of the Princess Dewa Ammajee. His Highness was only fifteen years of age when he thus became his own master and the sovereign of Coorg. His education, in the European sense of the word, had been entirely neglected; but he was a proficient in all Coorg accomplishments, being an excellent rider, a good shot, and a dexterous gymnastic. Young and inexperienced in public affairs, he intrusted the details of government, external and internal, to the management of his late father's Minister, Buswopah, an old and attached friend of the family, and to whose care his father, when dying, had especially confided him. Leaving, therefore, all business to this Minister, the Rajah spent the greatest part of his time in field sports, for which the forests and wilds of his country afforded him peculiar facilities and ample space, in reviewing his troops, or in receiving the visits of foreigners of distinction.

His regular army consisted, at this time, of about 10,000 infantry, and 1000 irregulars, besides 100 pieces of cannon distributed among the different forts and passes. In cases of emergency, also, every Zemindar fully equipped at his own expense, with matchlock, sword, and shield, was liable to military service during the continuance of hostilities.

Justice was administered by means of magistrates, who were chosen from among the land proprietors. In cases involving capital punishment, that of decapitation, sentence was pronounced by the Brahmins, in accordance with the Shasters; but the Rajah could revoke the sentence at will. All religions were tolerated at Coorg, but the most prevailing one was a species of the Hindu. Idol worship was also practised.

In 1830 the Rajah, who was at that time twenty-six years of age, was seized with a violent illness; and it being supposed that a surgical operation would be necessary, Mr. Jeaffreson, an eminent surgeon in the service of the Hon. East India Company, was summoned from Bombay, to attend his Highness. Having obtained permission from the authorities so to do, that gentleman, accompanied by Capt. Hill, of H.M.'s 54th Regt., set out for Mercara, where he at length arrived, after a tedious and somewhat perilous journey on horseback up the mountains. Fortunately he found that there was but little or no occasion for the employment of his professional skill, the account of the Rajah's malady having been much exaggerated, so that he had scarcely anything else to do than to enjoy the hospitality of his illustrious and generous host. With Mr. Jeaffreson's kind permission we give the following interesting description of his visit, as communicated by that gentleman, in a letter to a friend:—

"DEAR S.—Upon our arrival at the palace we were presented to the Rajah, who received us in the most cordial manner, assuring us that, like his ancestors, he entertained a particular regard and esteem for Englishmen.

"The interview concluded, we were conducted to a garden outside the palace, in which the wildness of Indian mountain scenery was agreeably contrasted with the elegancies of modern horticulture. There we found a splendid bungalow, fitted up for our accommodation, with every possible convenience.

"Round this residence grew flowers of the richest hues and the sweetest perfume, while trees, laden with delicious fruit, among whose branches perched wild birds of the brightest and most variegated plumage, cast over us their agreeable shade.

"Near this bungalow was a tank, made of black marble of the highest polish and most elaborate workmanship, in the centre of which rose a fountain, throwing up jets of water so clear and pellucid that hundreds of large and beautiful fish might be seen disporting in the basin, or else darting about in every direction after their prey. This tank was the favourite resort of the Rajah, who was wont to visit it daily, at noon. Standing beside it, he would ring a small gold bell, he carried in his hand, and, at its tinkling, all the fish collected together in one spot, anxiously awaiting their food (young frogs, parched peas, &c.), which an attendant threw to them from a basket.

"In another part of the garden was an immense black marble stand, of pyramidal form, along the five front steps of which were ranged hundreds of bleached skulls of elephants, being the *opima spolia* of the chase.

"The Rajah was about the middle size, and by his muscular and well-knit frame, seemed formed by nature to excel in those athletic sports in which he still takes so much delight. His physiognomy was at once prepossessing and intelligent; his nose aquiline; his eyes large, bright, and expressive; and his whole demeanour bespoke dignity and command.

"The Rajah is a graceful and fearless horseman, an unerring shot, and wields his favourite weapons, the sword and the spear, with great dexterity and address; he is also a swift runner, although upon one occasion I had the good fortune of bearing off the palm from him in a foot-race; as for wrestling, I have no doubt that, were his Highness 'to try a fall' with one of our Lancashire or Westmoreland lads, he would come off victorious; he is also a good draughtsman, and has an excellent ear for music, of which he is particularly fond, having kept in his pay, at Coorg, a regular band of European performers, whose ability would command attention even in a London concert-room. Within the palace was a large and well arranged armoury, where might be seen specimens of every description of weapon, offensive and defensive, from those of remote antiquity down to the modern rifle. The Rajah took great delight in exhibiting this collection. His Highness often condescended to amuse us by giving us proofs of his skill and address in athletic exercises, thus showing a strong contrast to many other Indian princes, who, abandoned to effeminacy and dissolute pleasures, pass their time in the harem, surrounded by eunuchs, and given up *et Veneri, et cœnis et plumis Sardanapali.* We were particularly gratified at, finding that this prince, who could, if necessary, have brought into the field a well-appointed army of 25,000 men, was easy of access to his ryots, listening patiently to their grievances, and manifesting towards them the utmost consideration and kindness; this ensured him, in return, their loyalty and affection; as a proof of which, whenever we travelled with the Rajah, into the interior of the country, hundreds of natives, men, women and children—who, from curiosity, crowded round my companion and me,—an Englishman being a *rara avis* in those parts—received the Rajah with every demonstration of respect and attachment. It gives me the greatest satisfaction to mention this, being aware that the most sinister reports have, for interested purposes, been industriously propagated to the Rajah's prejudice. Another fact, also, I think it my duty to state, in disproof of such calumnies. Before leaving Bombay, several persons residing there, and who had received intelligence that some of their relatives in Coorg had been unjustly and most cruelly put to death by the Rajah, desired me to make inquiries as to the truth of such reports. This I did; and it was with the greatest pleasure I obtained the surest proof of the falsehood of such allegations, by the appearance before me, in real flesh and blood, of the very parties who were said to have been so unceremoniously disposed of.

"Shortly after our arrival, I was suddenly awakened at midnight by my servant, who told me that the Rajah had sent for me. Apprehensive that his Highness might have been seized with sudden indisposition, I proceeded, in all haste, to the palace, and found, to my astonishment, that the Rajah had sent for Captain Hill and me to accompany him upon a hunting excursion. Mounting a tall shikaree (hunting) elephant, without a houdah, the Rajah, who himself performed the office of mahout or driver, desired Captain Hill and me to place ourselves behind him, no enviable situation, I can assure you, for us who had hitherto been accustomed only to the convenience and luxury of a palanquin. The night was dark and dreary, and the distance to the hunting rendezvous not less than twenty English miles. Arrived, about six o'clock in the morning, at the appointed spot, we found that several tents had been pitched and an excellent breakfast prepared for us, to which you may readily imagine, the keen air of the Coorg mountains, no less than the rough jolting of our *monture*, disposed us to do ample justice.

"Here the Rajah left us for a time, for the purpose, as he said, of superintending certain preparatory arrangements, which would occupy several hours, and proceeded towards another collection of tents in sight of ours, and containing, according to the custom of Eastern princes, some of his numerous wives, who, although concealed from view, could witness the sport.

"We were to be duly summoned when all was prepared. Now, considering that the forest had to be 'drawn,' as it is technically called; that above 5000 men, huntsmen and others, with every kind of implement, were to be employed in clearing away the thickset, closely entangled jungle, from an area of more than one square mile; that strong and powerful nets were to be placed in every rivulet, in order to prevent the escape of such elephants as were known to be located within a few miles of us—we did not regard eight or nine hours as too long a time for such operations; besides, we were the better reconciled to the delay, as it afforded us the opportunity of taking a sound nap, and of thus indemnifying ourselves for the loss of a night's repose.

"The anxiously expected signal was at length given; all was ready. On reaching the place indicated to us, we found that the jungle had been cut away and cleared for a considerable distance, and that two enormous trees, nearly in the centre of this rude circle, had been selected, from which a kind of capacious cradle, made of wickerwork, was suspended, well secured by strong ropes, at the height of from twenty to thirty feet from the ground, and into which, by means of a rope-ladder, the Rajah, Captain Hill, and I, deposited ourselves, accompanied by several attendants wearing green hunting uniforms, who had the care of and loaded various rifles of every kind, and by every maker. The Rajah, himself a most excellent marksman, courteously declined taking any other part in the sport than that of a spectator: in fact he had issued strict orders to his soldiers and others to load their guns with blank cartridges only, and not to shoot at any animal except in self-defence—his Highness's wish being to give us, his guests, all the credit of success. These preliminary arrangements completed, we had now only to await patiently for the enemy's approach. To beguile the time the Rajah recounted to us many of his 'hair-breadth 'scapes i' the imminent deadly' jungle (that most perilous of all hunting fields), proving that, if the pleasure of the sport be indeed great, it is often purchased at the risk of life or limb, and requires, in the bold amateur, the utmost coolness and resolution.

"Soon the report of volleys of musketry, intermingled with the clangour of trumpets, the beating of drums, the yells and hootings of the huntsmen, and the roaring of the beasts they were driving before them, announced that the hunt had commenced. It was, indeed, a most exciting moment, and one which can only be conceived by those who have already witnessed such a scene. In proportion as the radius of the circle diminished, these sounds increased in intensity, and we could, at length, descry in the distance, hundreds of wild animals of every kind; but we were advised to reserve our fire for our expected guests, who soon made their appearance in the shape of twelve elephants, one of them being of immense size and uncommon beauty. 'I should like that one,' said the Rajah, pointing to it, 'to be taken alive, as a present for the Governor-General.' We assured his Highness that his wish should be complied with, and then commenced our attack, the result of which was that the other elephants, with the exception of one which contrived to make his escape, soon fell, pierced by our rifle balls, six to my share and four to that of Captain Hill, leaving the twelfth, the elephant in question, our prize.

"About thirty tame elephants, trained to pass ropes round the legs of the captive, immediately surrounded him, and seemed to say, 'You are our prisoner,' a fact of which, indeed, the poor animal's sorrowful but still indignant look showed him to be but too cognizant.

"Thus secured, we escorted him to prison, preceded by a band of music, and followed by the Rajah's numerous retainers; and in this manner ended a hunt, in which Capt. Hill and myself can boast of carrying off a heavier game-bag than falls to the lot of most sportsmen—ten elephants. I am perfectly aware of the absolute necessity that there is for the destruction of these magnificent animals—the ravages they commit in the sugar plantations (the sugar-cane is their favourite food) being to an enormous and ruinous extent; but, nevertheless, when I consider their docility, their sagacity (so great as to have gained them the epithet of *half-reasoning*), and their many other excellent qualities, I am determined, should I again visit India, never more to aim a rifle at them. With the ferocious and blood-thirsty tiger the case is different: he is the ruthless enemy and destroyer of our race, and him I can pursue to the death with the utmost satisfaction.

"I was particularly gratified, therefore, on a subsequent day, when, accompanied by the same princely *cortège*, I shot the largest royal tiger I ever beheld, which was brought home and exhibited, by torch-light, in the court-yard of the palace, and decorated with evergreens, and other appropriate emblems of the chase, the band playing, the inhabitants being admitted and marching round in procession, and the Rajah's wives, no doubt, peeping at the royal show from the windows of the harem: the sight was, indeed, at once novel and exciting to us. The sports were frequently varied, and on several occasions the Rajah took us, on moonlight nights, to different concealed retreats in the dense forests, at a considerable distance from the palace. The jungle had been cleared in front of these retreats, and tempting food (the flesh of various animals) was regularly, for many nights successively, strewed about. These temporary buildings being formed of logs of timber, covered with brushwood, had several loopholes large enough to admit the muzzles of our rifles, enabling us, also, to see the cautious arrival of various animals, their gambols, &c. In these places we secreted ourselves before nightfall, and not even a whisper was permitted. At a given signal we all fired simultaneously at such animals as we had selected for our sport; such as escaped would not, of course, return, perhaps, for many nights, consequently we all adjourned to another *cachette* of the same construction, but at some considerable distance off. Not the least interesting part of the night's sport was that of watching the manœuvres of these animals, consisting of tigers, wild boars, chitas, jackals, &c. &c. Some of these animals, although the natural prey of one another, could not resist joining company at this sumptuous banquet, and entering, as it were, into a truce by mutual consent, at the same time compelling each other to observe a respectful distance by means of snarling and howling in the most hideous manner.

"After twenty-two days' stay with the Rajah—days replete with amusement, pleasure, and interest, and which I shall ever remember with unmixed satisfaction—the time arrived for our leaving Coorg.

"Upon the evening preceding our departure, Captain Hill and myself proceeded to the palace to take our leave of his Highness, the Captain being in full regimentals. The Rajah's body-guard, a guard of honour, and the band, were all drawn out on the occasion. On our arrival, the soldiers presented arms, the band playing, 'God save the King,' in very good style, a compliment to which Captain Hill responded by giving his Highness the military salute, and I, by shaking him heartily by the hand. When we bade the Rajah farewell, his Highness was visibly affected; a dead silence ensued for some minutes, while sorrow was imprinted on every brow. It seemed as if we had a presentiment that our next meeting would not be a happy one; and so it proved, for the very next year the Rajah's troubles commenced. Of the subsequent events connected with his Highness, his deposal by the Hon. East India Company, his eighteen years' detention at Benares, and his visit to England, where he is now residing, respected and beloved by all who have the honour of his acquaintance, I need not speak, as they are already known to you. I shall therefore conclude by assuring you, &c.,

"Wm. Jeaffreson."

We now approach the particular subjects which are connected with, and, in fact, led to, the unhappy differences between the Company and the Rajah, and ended in war being declared against him.

In the lifetime of the Rajah's father and mother, one of his sisters was married to a person named Chen Buswah, chosen out of the body of the people, for he had no hereditary connection with the royal family of Coorg. That sister died, and the entreaties of the ladies of his family subsequently induced the Rajah, although much against his own inclination, to consent to Chen Buswah's marriage with another sister, called by the same name, Dewa Ammajee, as her aunt, the late Ranee of Coorg, in order to prevent what would have been considered a degradation to the family, by Chen Buswah marrying any person of inferior rank. Chen Buswah and his wife lived a short distance from the capital, in a manner befitting their station and connection with the royal family, the means of maintaining their social position being provided by the Rajah. Some time after the second marriage, and in the year 1832, Chen Buswah became dissatisfied with what he considered his subordinate condition, and, giving way to ambitious views, meditated nothing less than to dethrone the Rajah. Foiled, however, in this his wicked attempt, he determined upon escaping, with his wife and followers, to the British frontier; to effect which, he one night drugged the two officers in attendance upon him, bound one of them hand and foot, and suspended him from the rafters of the house, where he was afterwards found dead. His next step was to send on persons before him, to announce that it was the Rajah himself who was travelling *incog.* with the ladies of his family, and that no person was to appear in the roads while the *cortège* was passing. By this stratagem the roads were cleared for his advance, and he was thus enabled to reach as far as the barrier between Coorg and the Mysore country, without being observed or molested. On arriving there, the jemadar, or officer in command of the post, suspecting something wrong, advanced towards the party, and discovered Chen Buswah. The jemadar thereupon, acting according to his orders, refused to allow him to pass the barrier, unless he had the Rajah's permission to leave the country. An altercation ensued, and Chen Buswah shot the jemadar dead on the spot. The jemadar's brother, one of the guard, instantly levelled his matchlock at Chen Buswah, but before he could discharge it, he also was killed by one of the followers of Chen Buswah, who in the confusion escaped with his party into the Mysore country.

These facts were speedily communicated to the Rajah, and many of his subjects came forward, and offered to bring back Chen Buswah, dead or alive, from Mysore. This offer he declined: relying on the good faith of the Company, and on the friendly alliance, resting on treaty, which existed and had been so long kept up between that Government and the Sovereigns of Coorg, he wished that the former would deliver up Chen Buswah on his being demanded. A friendly communication was accordingly made by him to the Resident of Mysore, who was at the time at Yelwall, his country seat, only thirty miles distant from the Coorg frontier, and where, as the Rajah heard, Chen Buswah was. A statement accompanied the demand, detailing the above circumstances, and the bodies of the murdered men were embalmed, to enable the Resident himself to see them, he being invited to ascertain the truth. The answer received was to the purport and effect, that the Company could not give up a person who had sought its protection, as Chen Buswah had done.

Being very much surprised by this answer, the Rajah addressed frequent letters, demanding Chen Buswah, in order that he might be tried for the murders with which he was charged.

So anxious was the Rajah to avoid a collision with his friends and allies, that he addressed the following letter to Mr. Jeaffreson, of the Hon. East India Company's service, the gentleman who had paid him the visit above described.

(*Translation.*)

"Murkaira.—Rajjab, 1248, Hegira. (March, 1832.)

"In the month of Zilhujja, 1246, Hegira (1830) you favoured me with a visit, and remained with me twenty-two days—an interval of time which afforded you a sufficient opportunity for observing my private character, as well as the system adopted by me in the government of my dominions.

"I now regret to inform you, that a misunderstanding has lately arisen between Mr. Casamajor, the Resident of Mysore, and myself, the occasion of which was as follows:—One Chen Buswah was living in Koyoung-garree Nur-appoo Gutta: he was a married man, and, in addition to having had a free grant of land from me, had received many proofs of my royal favour and kindness. This person, without any provocation whatsoever, and solely instigated by his own evil passions, collected together a number of armed followers, and, placing himself at their head, raised the standard of revolt, for the purpose of dethroning me.

"His attempt, however, proving unsuccessful, Chen Buswah fled, and escaped to the British frontier, having, previously to his so doing, cruelly tortured, and afterwards poisoned, a person who had offended him, besides having, during his flight, killed two men, and severely wounded one, who had endeavoured to intercept him.

"This atrocious criminal has, I am sorry to say, received protection from Mr. Casamajor, the British Resident at Mysore: a circumstance the more extraordinary, since, from the time that the friendship and alliance between the British Government and my ancestors first took place, we have been blended together, like sugar and milk, or, as you would express it, we have been hand-and-glove together, in short, almost one and the same state.

"The extradition of criminals was, in fact, a constant and invariable rule between us, and had, as is well known to every British officer, been established for a very long time. Acting, therefore, in perfect conformity therewith, I repeatedly wrote to Mr. Casamajor, requiring him to deliver up to me the said criminal; but although, in addition to so doing, I thrice sent persons duly authorized to demand and receive him, they as often returned empty-handed. I am sorry to say, that Mr. Casamajor still persists in his conduct, not even deigning to reply to my requisitions.

"I assure you, my dear sir, that the pain and mortification occasioned me by this circumstance have been very great, especially as I am, and always intend to be, the staunch and faithful ally of the British Government. But it must be evident to you, that the infringement of the above regulation will, by lessening the respect of my subjects for me, cause disaffection among them, and thus undermine the very foundations of my authority.

"I cannot express the regret I feel at having to trouble a British officer with my grievances; but how am I to maintain my character as an independent prince, if my legitimate authority be thus wrested from me?

"Having, however, whenever called upon, cheerfully come forward to assist the British Government with aid and reinforcements, I trust that I shall be treated by them in the manner such services merit.

"In conclusion, I beg of you, my dear sir, to advise me what I had best do in this matter. It is my sincere wish, I assure you, still to observe all the terms of the alliance with your Government as religiously as I have hitherto done; and all I ask for, in return, is a reciprocal observance of the same upon their part, and the consequent delivering up to me of Chen Buswah and his adherents.

"I entreat you, therefore, to use your influence in amicably arranging this untoward circumstance; and by so doing you will, at one and the same time, relieve me from great anxiety, and ensure my lasting esteem and gratitude.

"And now, what more can I say, than to desire you to consider me as your friend, and that you will continue to favour me, from time to time, with accounts of your health and welfare. (Signed) "VEER RAJUNDER WADEER.

"To Wm. Jeaffreson, Esq."

The answer from Mr. Jeaffreson was as follows:—

(*Copy.*)

"His Highness Samme Veer Rajunder Wadeer, Rajah of Coorg, &c. &c.

"HONOURABLE AND DEAR SIR,—I have been favoured with

your letter, and hasten to answer it, and sympathise with your Highness on the distress which the circumstance detailed in it must have occasioned, and which demands immediate justice to render your future reign glorious, secure, and happy, and which justice your treaty with the English nation entitles you to exact. I must, however, hope and believe, that there has been some misunderstanding, or want of proper explanation, withheld from the Resident of Mysore, or justice would have been dealt out to you, and the murderers who have taken shelter under his jurisdiction given up on a *regular* and *formal* request being made; for this is doubtless the first law of treaty between all nations, and one that the *English always* hold the most sacred and inviolable. It will afford me much satisfaction to render your Highness any aid, and, accordingly, I beg to introduce the bearer of this, by name Mohammed Ghyeasoodden Mooftee, a gentleman well acquainted with native law, as well as English manners and customs, and native courts. He will confer with your Highness, and point out the most easy way to gain redress for your past wrongs, as well as to prevent a recurrence of them in future. My friend will obey your instructions, and communicate your Highness's pleasure to me. In the mean time, I beg to assure your Highness that I shall ever remain

"Your sincere friend and well-wisher,

(Signed) "W. Jeaffreson.

"Bombay, 12th Jan., 1833."

The well-meant and friendly endeavours of Mr. Jeaffreson were of no avail; and, as time passed on without any attention to the Rajah's representations and remonstrances, he became irritated to such a degree, as to write to the British authorities in a style and tone which has since caused him much pain. Other circumstances also occurred about the same time to widen the breach. The Rajah, who took great delight in seeing Englishmen, opened up Coorg by public roads; and, to render these more attractive to British travellers, erected bungalows at proper intervals, where they were not only entertained at his cost, but occasionally presented with gifts of considerable value. This profuse generosity led to abuses: the Resident of Mysore interfered, and orders were issued to prevent travellers from passing through Coorg without permission of the British authorities. This proceeding, which appeared to the Rajah a very arbitrary one, originated many angry discussions and disputes.

Nearly two years now passed, during which the breach was still further widened by disaffected persons, who, coming from Mysore, urged the Rajah to bid defiance to the East India Company, assuring him that he would receive powerful aid from that country, where, it was well known, disaffection existed. The conduct of the Company also, in stopping, as they now did, the payment of the interest due to him as their creditor and holder of their public securities, exasperated the Rajah still further; so that it cannot be wondered at, if, yielding to the representations and advice of his Minister, Buswapah, he ordered the barriers to be strengthened, abattis to be formed, stockades to be erected, and every possible means of defence to be prepared.

Whatever may be the opinion formed of the Rajah's policy in thus braving so powerful an adversary, it is certain, from what is laid down by Vattel and other eminent jurisconsults, that he had an undoubted legal right, both by the law of nations, and particularly the customs recognised and acted upon by friendly and allied states, to demand the extradition of Chen Buswah, in order that he might be tried for the crimes laid to his charge, in the country where it was alleged he had committed them.

Matters continued in this unsatisfactory state until about the close of the year 1833, or the beginning of 1834, when the Madras Government deputed one of its members, Mr. Græme, to proceed to Mercara, for the purpose of discussing the matter in dispute, and, if possible, of settling it amicably; but, most unfortunately, severe illness prevented the Rajah from receiving that gentleman, who, in consequence, returned to Bangalore.

It was not long after this that a person, calling himself Canara Menon, arrived at the capital of Coorg. He stated that he had come there, according to instructions, to meet Mr. Græme; but, not being furnished with the proper credentials, the Rajah believed him to be a spy, and caused him to be arrested as such, intending to detain him as a hostage, in order to compel the Company to do him (the Rajah) justice, by delivering up Chen Buswah.

On becoming aware of this person's detention, Mr. Græme caused a demand to be made for his immediate release; and it was then, for the first time, that the Rajah understood that Menon was Mr. Græme's vakeel. A lengthened and ineffectual correspondence ensued; neither party would yield, and the Company, of course, supported their Resident, both in his refusal to deliver up Chen Buswah, and in his demand to have Canara Menon released unconditionally. On the 17th of February, 1834, the Rajah received a letter from Lord W. Bentinck, the Governor-General, in which, after remonstrating with his Highness on the impropriety of his conduct, his lordship adds :—

"But the deep interest which the British Government has long felt in the welfare of the Coorg state, *the kind friendship and excellent services rendered by your ancestors* and predecessors to the Government, as well as the recollection of the circumstances attending *the connection of the two states, which since its commencement has been equally honourable to both*, still leads me to carry forbearance to the utmost limit. *My feelings towards you are those of parental kindness and solicitude;* and I still venture to entertain an expectation of your return to better feelings, and that recourse to hostile operations may yet be averted.

"It is my intention to proceed in a few days on my projected visit to Mysore, and I hope to reach Bangalore about the 25th instant. It will afford me sincere pleasure if, on my arrival there, I shall receive a friendly answer. I trust that you will be enabled to acquaint me of your having released Karoonagara Menon, and forwarded him and his attendants in safety to the Company's territories. If this difficulty be removed, and satisfactory explanation on other points be afforded, negotiations may be again commenced, and that harmony which during a long period has so happily subsisted between the states may continue uninterrupted."

The Rajah, acting, unfortunately, under the influence of evil counsellors, did not allow this kind letter to change his determination. The consequence was, that a peremptory demand was then made, intimating that, unless Canara Menon was released within six days, and sent in safety to the Mysore frontier, the Company would cease to treat the Rajah as a friend and ally, and that hostilities would be forthwith commenced against him. Accordingly, soon after the expiration of the specified time, the following proclamation was issued by the Governor-General, declaring his Highness to be deposed, and his country annexed to the Company's dominions.

The East India Company's Proclamation.

The conduct of the Rajah of Coorg has, for a long time past, been of such a nature as to render him unworthy of the friendship and protection of the British Government.

Unmindful of his duty as a ruler, and regardless of his obligations as a dependent ally of the East India Company, he has been guilty of the greatest oppression and cruelty towards the people subject to his government, and he has evinced the most wanton disrespect of the authority of, and the most hostile disposition towards the former, from whom he and his ancestors have invariably received every degree of kindness and protection.

It would be needless to enumerate the several instances of his misconduct; but it is sufficient to state that, in consequence of an asylum having been afforded in the British territories to his own sister, Dewammaji, and her husband, Channa Basavappa, who, to preserve their lives, had fled from his oppression, the Rajah has presumed to address letters replete with the most insulting expressions to the Governor of Fort St. George and the Governor-General of India; that he has assumed an attitude of hostility and defiance towards the British Government; that he has received and encouraged the proclaimed enemies of that Government; and that he has unjustifiably placed under restraint an old and faithful servant of the Company, named Kulputty Karnikara Manoon, who had been formally deputed by the British representative for the purpose of opening a friendly negotiation, thus committing a gross outrage, not only upon the authority by whom the above-named individual was deputed, but upon the established rules of all civilized nations, by whom the persons of accredited agents are invariably held sacred.

The ancient alliance and the firm friendship which had so happily subsisted between the predecessors of the present Rajah and the Honourable Company, have caused his errors to be treated uniformly with indulgence; the most earnest remonstrances have been in vain tried to bring him to a sense of his obligations; and it is not until further forbearance would be culpable, that his Excellency the Right Honourable the Governor in Council of Fort St. George, has resolved on employing the only means left of vindicating the dignity of the sovereign state, and of securing to the inhabitants of Coorg the blessings of a just and equitable government.

It is accordingly hereby notified, that a British army is about to invade the Coorg frontier; that Virarajendra Wodear is no longer to be considered as Rajah of Coorg; that the persons and property of all those who conduct themselves peaceably, or in aid of the operations of the British troops, shall be respected; and that such a system of government shall be established as may seem best calculated to secure the happiness of the people.

It is also hereby made known to all British subjects who may have entered the service of Virarajendra Wodear, that they are required to place themselves under the protection of the British authorities, by whom they will be kindly received, and their rights and privileges respected; and that such of them as may in any way render assistance to the enemy will be considered as traitors, and punished accordingly.

This proclamation will be carefully made known in Chittledrog, Raidroog, Mysore, Malabar, and Canara, in order that the relatives of such persons as have taken service in Coorg, from those places or adjoining districts, may adopt the earliest means of communicating its purport to the parties in whose safety they are interested.

(Signed) J. S. Fraser,
Lieut.-Col. and Political Agent of His Excellency
the Right Hon. the Governor-General.

Issued at Bangalore, this 15th day of March, 1834.

The die being now cast, the Rajah, in addition to his other preparations, addressed proclamations to the people in the Company's territories, calling upon the Hindoos and Mussulmans to rise, under the banners of the Haleri dynasty, against the foreign despots, who aimed at the spoiling of castes, and the destruction of the religion of Hindostan.

For the following fair, able, and interesting account of the operations of the British forces, which now advanced upon Coorg from the north, east, and west, we are indebted to Mr. Murray's *History of India*:—

"The Coorg country, as to its capacity of coping with the British power, might, from the small amount of its population, have been considered as utterly contemptible. The extreme difficulty of the ground, however, composed altogether of lofty mountains, covered with the thickest and most entangled jungle, defended by a race of determined valour, gave to it a somewhat serious character. A force of 6000 men was placed under Brigadier Lindsay, in whom was vested the supreme command of the expedition; and, marching from Mysore with the main body, he entered Coorg on the 1st of April. The troops were harassed by the difficulties of the road, which were much increased by large trees cut down and laid across it, so that they could scarcely accomplish above five miles in fourteen hours. The enemy, however, did not venture to encounter him, and all the stockades were found deserted. On the 6th, the army entered, without resistance, Mudakerry (Mercara), the capital, in which the British flag was displayed. The campaign thus seemed to have been easily and triumphantly terminated; and yet it acquired a somewhat disastrous character, from the operations of three other detachments, which entered the territory at different points.

"General Foulis, marching from Cannanore, on the western coast, approached, on the 2nd April, the entrance of the Hugul Ghaut, the principal opening from this side. The enemy had fortified it with three successive stockades, as well as with breastworks and felled trees, at every hundred yards. Their posts were driven in, and on the 3rd, at six in the morning, the attack began. The first stockade was carried with trifling loss; but from that time till four in the afternoon, a series of very hard conflicts was maintained in carrying the successive barriers, which the enemy defended with vigour, carrying on, at the same time, a continued skirmishing from the wood. The last stockade was only captured by attacking it in reverse, as well as in flank. Next day, as the colonel continued to advance, a flag of truce appeared, bearing a proposal from the Rajah for a suspension of arms. He replied, that if the Coorg troops did not fire, his would also abstain from doing so; but that nothing should prevent him from passing through the Ghaut. He accordingly effected this march without opposition, and in the afternoon arrived at Hugul. His service was now completed, with the loss of twelve killed and thirty-six wounded; but among the former was Lieutenant Erskine, a very promising young officer.

"At the same time, Col. Waugh, from the north, advanced upon a fortified position named Buck, seated on the brow of a steep ascent, and accessible only by a narrow defile, through a dense jungle. The assailing party was divided into two, who were each to make a detour and take the stockade in flank; but being misled, it is said, by native guides, they both met in front of that barrier. With characteristic valour, they rushed forward to the attack; but the place was so strong, and so vigorously defended, that all their efforts were vain, and their ranks were thinned by a most destructive fire. Upon encountering this resistance, the commander directed Lieut.-Colonel Mill to send part of his force to support the storming party; and immediately that officer, inspired by a too ardent valour, led them on himself, and was followed by the whole detachment. An impetuous assault was then commenced against the stockade; but being, in a great measure, built of stone, it baffled every attempt, while a most murderous fire issued from it against our countrymen. Mill was shot dead on the spot, and several, while vainly attempting to rescue his body, fell around him. Major Bird then determined to withdraw the party, and, with little additional loss, brought it under cover. In this most unfortunate affair, about 48 were killed, including three officers, and 118 wounded.

"Another column, under Lieutenant-Colonel Jackson, advanced from Mangalore upon a position named Bullary Pett; and this officer learning that there was a strong stockade five miles in front of him, sent Captain Noble with a detachment to reconnoitre it. The latter made his way through a narrow and winding path, till he arrived in front of the barrier; and, having completed his reconnaissance, he began his return, when a running fire was instantly commenced from among the bushes. His party continued exposed, during the whole of their retreat, to this assault from an invisible foe, whom they could neither elude nor repel; and the casualties amounted to 30 killed and 36 wounded.

"Colonel Jackson, after considering this loss, and the reported strength of the position, thought it impossible to attempt carrying the stockade without further reinforcements, and fell back upon Coombla."

It must, doubtless, appear singular to all who read the above narration, that Brigadier Lindsay should have been able to enter Mercara without encountering any opposition (the stockades having been deserted), while on every other point so desperate and successful a resistance had been made; but the fact is, that upon the Rajah's retiring to Nalkanader, the Dewans Bopu and Ponappa, who were left at Mercara, determined, in conjunction with their friends, to betray their unfortunate master, and surrender the capital to the Company. Accordingly the Dewan Bopu, with a party of 400 Coorgs, went to meet Colonel Fraser, the Agent of the Governor-General, and, after surrendering themselves to him, conducted the Company's troops to the capital.

The Rajah finding himself now in actual hostile collision with the British Government, whom he had been taught, from his childhood, to consider as the friend and protector of his family, became deeply distressed, and immediately despatched flags of truce to all the columns, thereby putting a stop, at once, to further bloodshed. It is evident, from the determined stand made at the stockades attacked by Lieutenant-Colonel Mill and Lieutenant-Colonel Jackson, that had his Highness allowed the fighting to continue, not only the loss to the British would have been much more severe, but the issue of the contest would have been doubtful, as the strongest stockades, barriers, and ghauts, were all in possession of the armed Coorgs, who were congregated in great force, and would have defended themselves to the last; besides which, the country had, at this time, risen to a man, and assembled in and around the capital.

Simultaneously with the sending of the flags of truce, the Rajah released Canara Menon, invested him with a khelat, or dress of honour, presented him with an elephant and many other valuable presents, and despatched him in all honour and safety to the British camp.

Upon the occupation of the capital by Brigadier Lindsay, Colonel Fraser, the Governor-General's Agent, sent a summons to the Rajah at Nalkanader, to come in and surrender, which, after a short delay only, he obeyed. Accordingly, on the night of the 23rd of April, 1834, accompanied by his whole family, a train of about 2000 attendants, mostly unarmed, and fifty palanquins containing his female establishment, he arrived at Mercara, and reoccupied his palace, where he remained a close prisoner.

On the 25th of April, Captain Carpenter had an interview with the Rajah at the palace, and informed him that he had instructions to conduct his Highness, as a state prisoner, together with his family, to Bangalore. A few hours after this communication, the Rajah and his whole family began their march, after having been required to surrender, and having accordingly surrendered, to the British authorities his treasure and valuables, amounting to about 15 or 16 lacs of rupees, or £150,000 or £160,000 sterling, his Highness and his family having been allowed to retain nothing more than their clothes and ornaments in actual use. Anxious to save something, if possible, from the rapacious hands of his conquerors, the Rajah had, at Sirtekote, the first halting-place, caused a pit to be dug, by those of his attendants in whom he placed the greatest confidence, in the ground on which stood the kitchen tent. In this pit he had deposited a considerable amount of gold he had managed to conceal in his own palanquin, and in those of his wives. After the gold had been so buried, and the men present made to swear a solemn oath to the Rajah, that they would faithfully keep the secret, the ground was again levelled, and kitchen fires lighted upon it. As might well be expected, the Rajah was almost immediately betrayed by one of his servants, a certain Mandria Uttaya of Nalkanader. This man, having secretly returned to the spot where the treasure was concealed, removed a considerable portion of it for his own use, intending to repeat his visits as opportunity might serve; but suspicions having been excited, on account of the quantity of gold in his possession, he was compelled to confess the whole affair; and the remainder of the treasure, having been recovered, was afterwards, together with the moneys and valuables above mentioned, distributed as prize money among the troops engaged in the expedition.

The melancholy march now proceeded for some time through the Rajah's own country, and if anything could add to its painful character, it was to see the inhabitants of the different villages through which it passed rushing out, crowding round their Rajah, and with every demonstration of sincere attachment lamenting his departure from among them.

As further proof of the esteem in which the Rajah was held by his subjects, it may be mentioned, that on his being deposed, as above, he issued a written order addressed to his Dewan, Soobadar, Moonshee, &c. &c., requiring them to state, in writing, the manner in which he had governed the country from the time of his assuming the reins of government up to his dethronement, and whether they were satisfied or not with his system of government.

The reply to this was a declaration signed by more than 400 persons, expressive of their entire satisfaction with the manner in which the Rajah had conducted his government and administered justice among them. This document is still in the possession of his Highness.

We add another equally important and convincing testimonial :—

"The following representation is made by the under-signed officials, Wallundar, and inhabitants of Coorg (here is inserted a long list of official titles, such as Curleka, Dewan, Shamlyn, &c.) in consequence of having been graciously desired to say, without fear or doubt, what system of government we wish to be established in Coorg, the Rajah Veer Rajundeer Wadeer being deposed.

"1. We do not wish that any substitute should be placed over us as a Rajah. We all consent to be governed according to the rules and customs of the British Government, if an English Sudar is placed over us to examine into our grievances and to protect us.

"2. The removal from this country to another place of Veer Rajundeer Wadeer, the descendant of that race which has, for so many generations, governed us and our forefathers, causes us pain and brings shame to us. *We therefore represent our grief to the British Government, and pray that the Rajah may be allowed to remain here, although deprived of all his power and authority.* We will still remain obedient to the great Government. In the time of the Sultan, the great Rajah and his subjects were strictly faithful servants of the Superior Government. *If, in the same manner, and as we have before petitioned, the Rajah is retained, and protected here, all the people of this country will greatly rejoice.* What more shall we state to those who know all things?

"Dated April 13, 1834."

On the 12th of May the Rajah and suite reached Bangalore; there he remained for some time a close prisoner, until removed to the Fort of Vellore, where he continued until the March following, when he and his family were escorted to Benares, in Hindostan, the place assigned as his future residence, an annual pension being given him of 60,000 rupees, or £6000 sterling.

Let us here pause to ask if the East India Company were

justified in this their severe treatment of the unfortunate Rajah. When the eminent services rendered to them by his ancestors, more especially by his illustrious uncle Veer Rajunder Wadeer, are considered—services but for which they never could have crushed the power of their mortal foe, Tippoo Sultan, surely some lesser punishment than the loss of his dominions, the plunder of his private treasures, and *even* the confiscation, contrary to the law of nations,[1] of his *funded* property, might have been meted out to him. Even Mr. Thornton, the paid historian and apologist of the Company's iniquitous deeds, is compelled to offer some apology for an act which the not very scrupulous Catherine II. would have hesitated to perpetrate. "The annexation," he observes, "of the conquered territory to the British dominions is not, in the first view, so clearly justifiable; but a very few words of explanation will show that, in this instance also, the right course was taken. The Rajah was childless, and he had taken effectual measures to cut off all pretensions to the succession not derived from himself." There can be no better answer to both these assertions than that the Rajah had a son, Prince Chitter Shuiker, who was born in the year 1832, and was consequently two years old at the time of his father's deposal. What then becomes of Mr. Thornton's attempt at whitewashing his patrons? But it was the Rajah's misfortune to be conquered by a corporation, a trading corporation, whose sole instinct is the *auri cœcus amor*, and whose moral responsibility being *nil*, is perfectly indifferent as to the meaus by which it accomplishes its ends.

For seventeen years the Rajah remained a state prisoner at Benares; with how much patience and dignity (qualities rarely found under such circumstances, except in a mind at ease with itself) he bore his severe misfortunes, the following letters will amply testify:—

[1] See Vattel's *Law of Nations*, **book ii. c. 18, s. 344.**

The Earl of Ellenborough, Governor-General of India, to his Highness Veer Rajunder Wadeer, Benares.

Allahabad, May 20th, 1841-3.

SIR,—I can assure you that I sympathise very sincerely with your Highness in the position in which you and your young family are placed.

Your Highness must be fully aware that there are public considerations which often prevent the indulgence of personal feelings, and that men placed in high stations are those who are least permitted to follow the dictates of the heart.

Before I can venture to decide upon your Highness's appeal to me, I must make myself acquainted with circumstances of which, in consequence of my recent arrival in India, I am not sufficiently informed, and I must communicate with the Governments of Madras and Bombay.

The concurrent testimony of all my countrymen, who have had the good fortune to become personally acquainted with your Highness, in favour of your character and conduct during your residence at Benares, much strengthens my own feelings of sympathy, and will make me very desirous that it should be found practicable to make some arrangement satisfactory to your Highness, and honourable to your exalted family.

I remain, with much regard and consideration,

Your Highness's faithful friend,

(Signed) ELLENBOROUGH.

Minute recorded by Lieut.-Colonel Carpenter, Agent to the Governor-General of India.

Benares, 1st January, 1848.

The period for my departure from Benares and return to Europe having arrived, I cannot part with his Highness the Rajah of Coorg without giving him a testimonial of the sentiments with which he has inspired me.

Since the Rajah quitted his palace in Coorg, in April, 1834, he has been under my charge, *and I have infinite satisfaction in recording the quiet, peaceable, and exemplary behaviour of his Highness, during the long period of nearly fourteen years that I have been a constant observer of his conduct, and which has been several times favourably noticed in my various reports to the Supreme Government.*

I am aware that, *subsequent to the Rajah's deposal,* numerous charges of cruelty and oppression, whilst he reigned in Coorg, have been brought against him; but I am bound in justice to declare, that, during the whole time he has been under my care, no evidence of a cruel disposition has ever been exhibited; on the contrary, his manners and habits are mild and gentle in the extreme, and he has invariably won the regard and esteem of all parties with whom he came in contact since he quitted Coorg. Unfortunately, previous to that event, he had never seen more than half a dozen European officers in his life. *The Rajah is a perfect specimen of an innate gentleman, though naturally reserved and shy, so that it becomes necessary to know him well to appreciate his many good and amiable qualities: he is particularly susceptible of attention and kindness.*

In conclusion, I earnestly recommend him and his family to consideration, and heartily and sincerely bid him farewell, with my best and warmest wishes that comfort and happiness may attend them in every situation, and under all circumstances. The Rajah's numerous children are especial objects of care and anxiety to him, owing to the extreme difficulty of providing for their future welfare, more particularly the little girl he is in the habit of dressing in the European style. Any kindness to her is peculiarly gratifying to the Rajah, and he is very desirous that she shall be educated and brought up as if she were an European: whatever arrangements he may wish to make for the future provision of the child, will, I trust, receive the assistance and support of my successor, as far as it may be in his power to grant it.

(Signed) T. D. CARPENTER,
Lieut.-Col. and Governor-General's Agent.

Cawnpore, November 8th, 1849.

MY DEAR RAJAH,—I was very sorry to find that I omitted, on the day of my departure from Benares, to bid you farewell. I can assure you that I separated from you with much regret; for during our intercourse, extending, as it did, over a period of upwards of eighteen months, *your mild and gentlemanlike manners, and your very correct conduct on all occasions, completely won my good opinion and esteem. I shall ever feel a deep interest in the welfare of yourself and family*, and I sincerely hope that the Court of Directors will sanction your proceeding to England, and your taking your daughter to that country to be educated there, because I think that a visit to England would prove a source of great amusement and pleasure to yourself, and an English education could not fail to be of the utmost advantage to your daughter.

I hope that you will write to me sometimes, for I should derive great pleasure in learning any particulars concerning yourself and your interesting family.

Mrs. Macgregor unites with myself in wishing you and yours every happiness; and I hope you will always consider me, my dear Rajah, your sincere friend,

(Signed) G. H. MACGREGOR.

In the year 1848, the Rajah applied to the local Government for leave of absence to visit England. This journey was projected with the view of accomplishing the object nearest to his heart, that of carrying with him his daughter, the Princess Gouramma, in order that, on her arrival in this country, she might be baptized, educated, and brought up in the Christian faith, and, at the same time, acquire English manners and

English habits. The letter addressed by the Rajah to the Governor-General, for leave of absence, was as follows :—

Benares, March 2, 1848.

My Lord,—I desire to address your lordship on a subject which is near my heart, although I feel it an impropriety on my part to enter into a detail of family matters.

My manner of life, by the blessing of God, and as man can testify, for the last fourteen years that I have been under the care and keeping of Government, has been without reproach. Colonel Carpenter knows this, he having been uniformly with me since I left my country; and, besides this, several gentlemen holding high offices at this place can give their testimony.

When I resided in my own country, I had a predilection for European customs; subsequently to my residence in this province, this impression has been confirmed; and, adverting to the principles of the Christian religion as taught by its Founder, it has become my anxious wish that my daughter should receive a Christian education in England.

But in this design I can receive no aid from those with whom I have affinity; and, situated as I am here, I am unable to effect it. My daughter has, for some time past, adopted English habits and manners. This is known to Colonel Carpenter and other officers resident at this station, who can testify to it, if necessary.

I am anxious that she should proceed to England, to be brought up at such a place and in such a manner as the daughter of an English nobleman would receive her education.

If her gracious Majesty Queen Victoria should extend her favour also to my daughter, my happiness would be complete.

I trust the British Government will not object to my daughter, through your lordship's gracious interposition, proceeding to England, suitably to her rank and condition. The love of a parent to his child is obvious. I place my confidence in your lordship's kindness, and state my request exactly as I wish. I am the first of native chiefs, your lordship will observe, who has made this proposition. My daughter's age is six years and six months; and at this tender age the good effects of education are more certain than at a later period. It is not a great matter for your lordship to assent to my request. We look to you for indulgent consideration. Believe me to be sincere in my well-wishes, and to be anxious for an early intimation of assent to my request.

I remain, &c.,

(Signed) VEER RAJUNDER WADEER,
Rajah of Coorg.

To the Right Hon. Earl Dalhousie,
Governor-General of India, &c.

After an interval of more than a year and a half, the Rajah received the Governor-General's reply. It was as follows:—

Translation of a Khurreeta (Letter) from the Most Noble the Marquis Dalhousie, Governor-General of India, to his Highness Rajunder Wadeer, Rajah of Coorg. Dated 21st August, 1849.

(After compliments:)—

I have much pleasure in acknowledging the receipt of your friendly letter, announcing your intention to proceed to England, together with a miniature of your daughter, whom I had the pleasure of meeting at Benares, and entertain great regard for her. The resemblance of this picture to the original is striking, and therefore gratifies me very much. With respect to your intention to visit England, I am unable to give you permission until I obtain the sanction of the Honourable the Court of Directors. In order to obtain their early sanction, I have communicated with the Honourable Court.

I hope you may always consider me your sincere friend and well-wisher, and continue to favour me with an account of your health and welfare.—I am, &c.,

(Signed) DALHOUSIE.

Above six months more elapsed before the arrival of the wished-for permission, which was conveyed in the following terms:—

From the Secretary to the Government of India, to the Superintendent of the Ex-Rajah of Coorg.

Foreign Department. From Supt. No. 25, dated 25th July, 1849, to do. No. 1487, dated 21st August, 1849.

Dated Fort William, 20th March, 1850.

SIR,—1. With reference to the correspondence on the subject of the wish of the Ex-Rajah of Coorg to send one of his daughters to England for the purpose of receiving a Christian education, and his desire to accompany her thither, I am directed by the Governor-General in Council to inform you that the Honourable the Court of Directors, to whom the matter had been referred, has been pleased to consent to the visit, and to sanction the Rajah's absence from India for one year, with the understanding, however, that the Government are to be put to no expense on his account.

2. You are requested to intimate to the Rajah the Honourable Company's decision, and to make such arrangements for his Highness' journey as he may desire, reporting the same for the information of the Government.—I have, &c.,

(Signed) H. M. ELLIOT.

As it occurred to the Rajah that his visit to England, determined upon for another and very different purpose, might afford him an opportunity of bringing before the Home Department of the Indian Government, certain pecuniary claims (to be hereafter explained), which he had against the East India Company, he communicated the circumstance, in writing, to the late Major Stewart, the Governor's agent at Benares, who suggested that, in order to prevent any doubts arising as to the openness and straightforward character of his (the Rajah's) proceedings, he should apprise the Local

Government of his intention so to do. In accordance with his advice, the Rajah formally intimated the same to the Governor-General of India, by the following letter which he despatched two months previous to his leaving Benares :—

Translation of an Extract of a Letter from his Highness the Rajah of Coorg, addressed to the Governor-General of India, and forwarded to Major Stewart, dated 8*th of October*, 1851 :—

"You are aware that I have taken leave to go to England, on account of my daughter. On my arrival in that country, I intend to represent there those of my circumstances which I have already done to your Government. I have, therefore, informed you on the subject, considering you as my great friend."

That this intimation duly reached the high authority for whom it was intended, is proved by the following translation of a letter from Major Stewart to his Highness the Rajah of Coorg, dated 10th October, 1851 :—

"Your letter, enclosing one to the address of the Governor-General, has been received, and its contents are known.

"In accordance to your wishes, the letter has been this day sent to his lordship."

It will be observed that, in the letter addressed by Mr. Elliot to Major Stewart, not the least intention is expressed of appointing any person to accompany the Rajah to England, an arrangement which could, therefore, only have been made at the suggestion of the Major: this will be fully evident from the following :—

Translation of a Letter from the Secretary to the Government, dated 11*th December*, 1850, *No.* 2835, *in reply to a Letter of this Residency, dated* 27*th ultimo, on the subject of the arrangement for the Departure of his Highness the Rajah of Coorg to England.*

"The Rajah should be informed, that he is deposed, and is under the charge of the Government agent at Benares, and it has been a matter of favour that permission is granted to his Highness to proceed to England. *The necessity of an Englishman accompanying the Rajah is also approved* by the Government: that man should be a gentleman, and possessing the confidence, and under the control of, the English Government. No other Englishman should be allowed to accompany the Rajah but the person who is selected by the Government, and *who may be going on a furlough* to England. An engagement should be entered into by that gentleman that he should return to India after a year with the Rajah. The expense of his journey should be incurred by the Rajah; and on the receipt of this letter the Rajah should be distinctly informed that the expense of his journey should be entirely incurred by him, and that no Englishman, without the approval of Government, shall be allowed to accompany him. The Agent of Government is directed to find out a gentleman for the above purpose, and to carry out those instructions with every precaution."

On the 4th of September, 1851, Major Stewart wrote to inform his Highness that Major Drummond, of the 3rd Bengal Light Cavalry, had been appointed to accompany him to England; and the Rajah, in his reply, dated the 9th of the same month, expressed his satisfaction at the selection of that gentleman by the Government; "for had I," observes his Highness, "of my own accord, engaged any other one for the purpose, I should have been obliged to incur the expense; but, as he is appointed by the Government, I am relieved from it, for which I am very grateful."

Major Stewart was determined that the Rajah should not remain long in his agreeable error, and wrote the very next day to say that his Highness was much mistaken in supposing that he, the Rajah, would incur no expense on account of

Major Drummond, for that, on the contrary, he must bear all his charges, and that, if his Highness was not disposed to pay them, he, Major Stewart, would report his refusal to the Government, and prevent his going to England.

As if conscious that this selection of Major Drummond, his particular friend, and who, be it observed, was *not going on furlough*, might afterwards become the subject of animadversion, Major Stewart most disingenuously endeavoured to make it appear that he had mentioned the name of Major Drummond to the Government authorities, at the Rajah's particular request, an assertion which his Highness denied most emphatically. The Rajah now requested Major Stewart to inform him what would be the nature and amount of the charges he was to incur on Major Drummond's account. The Resident, as if desirous of leaving his friend as wide a margin as possible, declined giving an explicit answer, but took the opportunity of notifying to his Highness that he would also have to defray Mrs. Drummond's passage to England.

The Rajah, naturally indignant at such an imposition, remonstrated with Major Stewart upon the subject, representing to him that as he (the Rajah) had already selected competent female attendants for his daughter, he had no need whatever for Mrs. Drummond's services. His expostulations, as might be expected, were again met by the threat of his journey being prevented, and he had, therefore, no alternative but to acquiesce.

Major Stewart subsequently notified to the Rajah that the expenses he would have to defray for Major Drummond were:

	£	s.	d.
One year's salary, at £80 per month,	£960	0	0
Passage money from Benares to Calcutta,	25	0	0
Do. from Calcutta to London,	128	0	0
Do. for Mrs. Drummond,	128	0	0
Do. for Major D.'s return to India,	135	0	0
Total,	£1376	0	0

If a desire to oblige his friend may be urged as an excuse for Major Stewart, in thus saddling the unfortunate Rajah with such an expense for a twelvemonth's trip to England, surely there can no justification be found for the East India Company's having sanctioned so monstrous a charge—a charge still further increased by an item of £395. 6*s*. 1*d*. for hotel charges, made by Major Drummond, as incurred by him at Mivart's establishment in London, where he and Mrs. Drummond had remained from the 28th of May, 1852, to the 2nd of May, 1853.

A memorial, from which the preceding facts are extracts, was forwarded, on the 16th December, 1856, to the Court of Directors of the Hon. East India Company, praying them to take the matter into their own hands, so as to render it unnecessary for the Rajah to have recourse to legal measures for compelling Major Drummond to refund the money he had deducted from the Rajah's allowance, for the expenses he (the Major) had incurred at Mivart's Hotel, the amount of which, as before stated, was £395. 6*s*. 1*d*.

By a letter dated the 9th March, 1857, the Court of Directors decline acceding to the Rajah's request, enclosing, at the same time, the copy of a letter from Major Drummond, purporting to be a reply to the Rajah's memorial.

Major Drummond commences by stating that he was, by no means, the first individual proposed by Major Stewart, to the Rajah; for that several gentlemen, and especially Major Sandeman, had been named, but rejected by his Highness. That Major Sandeman was to have received from the Rajah 20,000 rupees, for accompanying him to England, but that the Major declined the appointment, induced so to do (to use his own words), "by the disingenuousness of the Rajah, and the foreshadowing of the consequences." Now, the fact is, that Major Sandeman had promised, provided the Rajah would consent to his accompanying him to England upon the above terms, to reinstate him on his throne, by legal means; when, however, the Rajah pressed him to sign a formal document to that effect, he declined so doing. Thus the intended engagement was at an end, and hence the charge of *disingenuousness* brought by the Major against the Rajah.

Major Drummond is wholly silent as to four most important facts:—1. That he (Major Drummond) was the intimate friend of Major Stewart. 2. That he (Major Drummond) *was not going on a furlough to England*, which was one of the *provisos* of the Indian authorities. 3. That Major Stewart threatened the Rajah, if he did not acquiesce in Major Drummond's appointment, he would inform the Governor-General of his refusal, and prevent his going to England at all. 4. That Major Drummond was a perfect stranger to the Rajah before he came to Benares.—As to Mrs. Drummond's appointment, the Rajah, having already engaged proper female attendants for his daughter, could not possibly have any reason for saddling himself with this fresh expense. He therefore remonstrated with Major Stewart upon the subject; but was again met with the same threat, that he should not proceed to the British shores unless he complied with this fresh item.

Major Drummond quotes a demi-official letter of his friend, in which Major Stewart says, "I beg to state that hotel expenses, both for you and Mrs. Drummond, as long as she had charge of the Rajah's daughter, were expressly considered part of the expenses to be defrayed by him during the time of his absence from Benares."

If such was indeed the case, it may be naturally asked, why did Major Stewart, when the Rajah wrote to him to inquire what his expenses would really be, reply, in his letter of the 24th September, 1851, "I cannot describe with accuracy what will be incurred for Major Drummond in England"?

In order to prove that the Rajah was aware that he should have to pay the said hotel charges, Major Drummond produces the copy of a deed lodged in Major Stewart's office, purporting to have been entered into by the Rajah, and stating that "further (that is in addition to the monthly salary of 800 rupees), he would have to pay all travelling, hotel, and other expenses." No such deed was ever signed by the Rajah, and he challenges Major Drummond to produce either the original or a duly authenticated copy of it.

The fact of the Rajah's paying the hotel charges at Calcutta, and even in London, so long as Major Drummond remained in his company, is no proof that he had bound himself to do so; still less is it a justification for the Major's continuing to run up fresh expenses at the hotel after the Rajah had left it.

Major Drummond asserts that the Rajah has laid himself open to a charge of inconsistency, because in his letter of the 20th December, 1852, he stated "that, with the exception of 800 rupees (£80) per month, the Rajah is not aware that he has to incur any other expense on account of Major Drummond, either as hotel charges or otherwise," while in Major Drummond's note of the 24th of July, 1852, or five months previously, distinct reference was made to hotel and other expenses on account of the Rajah.

Major Drummond here puts a very forced construction on the Rajah's words, by making them appear to say, that he (the Rajah) did not know of any such charges having been made by the Major; whereas the obvious meaning of his Highness was, that he was not aware that his defraying of such charges formed any part of the original engagement between the parties.

The hotel charges in question were incurred by Major Drummond after the Rajah had quitted the hotel (Mivart's), where Major Drummond still continued to remain, although the Rajah offered him suitable accommodation in the residence he had engaged at Brompton, and notwithstanding that, as his Highness was under his charge, it was his duty to be as near him as possible.

Lastly, Major Drummond endeavours to account for his refusal to submit his accounts to the Rajah, by stating that he considered it his duty to forward them to the Governor-General's agent at Benares.

It appears, however, that the Major acted prematurely in so doing, and that his Honourable Employers took a far different view of the matter, since by their letter of the 14th September, 1854, they directed him to forward to the Rajah a copy of the said account.

It was mentioned at page 68, that one of the Rajah's motives for coming to England was the prosecution of certain pecuniary claims he had against the East India Company. The nature of those claims is as follows.

At the time the Rajah surrendered himself and family to Colonel (now General) James S. Fraser, he was a creditor of the East India Company's Government to a very large amount, as the holder of public stock of that Government, being part of their funded Indian debt, secured by, and the principal and interest payable out of, their territorial revenues. This public stock was represented by certain Government securities, or Government promissory notes, in the nature of Exchequer Bills, and called, Company's paper. Part of that stock actually stood in the books of the Hon. East India Company, and part of the said securities was actually made out, in the individual name of the Rajah.

The money so invested in, and secured by, Government securities was originally lent to the Company's Government in divers amounts, and at divers times, by the late Veer Rajundur Wadeer, paternal uncle of the Rajah, and by the late Ling Rajundur Wadeer, his father, both formerly and successively Rajahs of Coorg. The late Rajah Ling Rajundur Wadeer succeeded his brother the Rajah Veer Rajundur Wadeer, and the now deposed Rajah again succeeded, on the death of his father, which happened in the year 1821, by right of inheritance, to the sovereignty of Coorg, as the sole heir and representative by Hindoo law.

The Rajah was accordingly, at the time of the occupation of

his country by British troops, entitled to, and held, the said Government stock and Government securities. These he had for some considerable time previously held and continued to hold without any doubt or suspicion, placing confidence in the good faith of the Company's Government, and feeling safe under the security and protection of the law of nations, the principles of which the Company's Government, in common with all civilized Governments, respect and observe.

One of those Government securities held by his Highness, and which had been made out in his own individual name, was to secure the payment to him of the sum of 203,900 sicca rupees, the equivalent of which in British sterling money is £22,938, together with interest payable thereon in the mean time, and half yearly, at and after the rate of £4 per cent. per annum.

The Government security was dated 1st May, 1832, and registered as No. 1733 of the Government Four per Cent. Loan of 1832-3. The following is a copy of this voucher:—

Fort William, the 1st of May, 1852.

Promissory note at four per cent. for 203,900 Calcutta sicca rupees. Registered at the Accountant-General's Office, No. 1733, of 1832-33.

(Signed) J. ALEXANDER,
Accountant-General.

The Governor-General in Council does hereby acknowledge to have received from Veer Rajundur Wadeer, Rajah of Coorg, the sum of 203,900 Calcutta sicca rupees, as a loan to the Honourable the United Company of Merchants of England trading to the East Indies, and does hereby promise, for and on behalf of the said United Company, to repay the said loan, by paying the said sum of 203,900 sicca rupees, to Veer Rajundur Wadeer of Coorg, his executors or administrators, or his or their order, on demand at the General Treasury at Fort William, after the expiration of three months' notice of payment to be given by the Governor-General in Council, in the Government Gazette, and to pay the interest accruing on the said sum of 203,900 sicca rupees at the rate of four per cent. per annum, by half-yearly payments, at the General Treasury of Fort William, to the said Veer Rajundur Wadeer, Rajah of Coorg, his executors or administrators, or his or their order, until the expiration of three months after such notice of payment aforesaid, when the amount of interest will be payable with the principal, and such notice being considered as equivalent to a tender of payment, at the period appointed for the discharge of this note all further interest shall cease. The Governor-General in Council hereby further engages that the said loan shall not be paid off before the 1st of May, 1834.

Signed, by the authority of the Governor-General in Council,

H. J. PRINCE,
Secretary to the Government.

Received in cash the twelve months' interest due on this note from 1st May, 1832, to the 1st May, 1833, sicca rupees (8156) eight thousand one hundred and fifty-six.

Previous to the last-mentioned date, his Highness, as sole heir-at-law and representative by Hindoo law of his deceased father, the said Rajah Ling Rajundur Wadeer, held another Government security, or Company's paper, registered as 3596 of 1822-3, and a like amount of Government stock in the Madras 5 per cent. loan. This amount, in and by that Government security, was acknowledged to have been received from the said Rajah Ling Rajundur Wadeer by the Governor in Council of Madras as a loan; and the Governor in Council, on behalf of the East India Company, promised to repay it to him, his executors or administrators, or to his or their order, with interest in the mean time payable half-yearly at the rate of 5 per cent. per annum. From the time of the death of his father, the Rajah received from the Madras Government the interest on this Government security as it accrued due and payable, the Government taking receipts from his Highness, on the back of the said security, for the interest from time to time paid to him according to usage, which receipts were granted in the Rajah's own individual name.

The Rajah was therefore acknowledged to be entitled to the said Government security, and the money thereby secured, in succession to his said father; and his Highness accordingly continued to receive such interest until the date hereinafter mentioned.

Notice was afterwards given by the East India Company's Government that the said 5 per cent. loan would be paid off, and the Rajah thereupon, instead of demanding and receiving payment of the amount of such last-mentioned Government security (which he was then entitled to, and would have undoubtedly received from the Madras Government), elected and agreed to transfer the amount due thereon to another loan called the 4 per cent. loan of the Bengal Government, of the 7th of June, 1831, and to receive a new Government security to secure a like amount of stock in that 4 per cent. loan, upon giving up such 5 per cent. Government security.

This transfer was accordingly effected through the Resident at Mysore, the political officer of the British Government, who alone was authorised and empowered to hold political relations and carry on all official communications with the Rajah, as sovereign of Coorg.

The Rajah, in pursuance of this agreement, delivered up the 5 per cent. Government security to that officer, who thereupon granted to his Highness a formal written acknowledgment, of which the following is a copy. That is to say:—

Mysore Residency, 20th December, 1831.

I hereby acknowledge that Veer Rajundur Wadeer, Rajah of Coorg, has this day transferred into the Honourable Company's treasury a promissory note 3596 of 1822-23 for

Calcutta sicca rupees, two lacs three thousand and nine hundred in favour of Ling Rajundur Wadeer, late Rajah of Coorg, for which he is entitled to receive a promissory note bearing interest from the 1st of May, 1832, of the tenor and subject to the conditions specified in the advertisement published in the Government Gazette of the 9th of June, 1831, and intermediately the same interest from the date of this acknowledgment to the 30th of April, 1832.

(Signed) J. H. CASAMAJOR, Resident.

The Rajah accordingly, in pursuance of that undertaking on the part of the Resident at Mysore, afterwards duly received the intermediate interest, due from the 20th December, 1831, to the 30th April, 1832, from the Madras Government; and in further pursuance of such undertaking on his part, and in consideration of having surrendered the former Government security, the Rajah received from the Bengal Government, a Government security of the 4 per cent. loan in his own individual name, which was the Government security first above mentioned.

On that substituted Government security the Rajah received the interest, by a special permission to that effect, from the Madras Government, that treasury being nearer to the Rajah's country than the Bengal treasury.

It will thus be seen that the title of the Rajah to this Government security, and to this principal money and interest secured thereby, was over and over again, and in fact throughout, acknowledged and admitted by the Company's Government.

A second of the Government securities, which the Rajah held previous to, and at the time of, the occupation of the capital of Coorg by the British troops, was a renewed Government security issued by the Governor of Madras in Council, registered No. 65 of 1828-29, of the 6 per cent. Madras Government loan, to secure the principal sum of Madras rupees 653,940 (£65,394), together with interest at the last-mentioned rate. The following is a copy of this Government security:—

Fort, St. George, 1st February, 1811.

Promissory Note for 653,940 *Madras Rupees.*

The Right Honourable the Governor in Council does hereby acknowledge to have received from *her Highness Dewa Ammajee, Ranee of Coorg,* the sum of Madras rupees 653,940, as a loan to the Honourable United Company of Merchants of England trading to the East Indies, and does hereby promise, for and on behalf of the said United Company, *to repay* and discharge the said loan by paying *unto the said her Highness Dewa Ammajee,* Ranee of Coorg, her *executors or administrators, or her or their order,* the principal sum of Madras rupees 653,940 aforesaid, at the Presidency of Fort St. George, agreeably to the order in which this note may stand on the register of notes and bonds of this Presidency, payable according to priority of date and number, according to the *condition of the advertisement published in the Madras Government Gazette of 2nd December,* 1809, and by paying the interest accruing thereon at the rate of *six per cent. per annum,* from the day of the date hereof, by half-yearly payments from year to year, in cash, at the General Treasury at the Presidency, until the principal shall be discharged.

Accountant-General's Office. Registered as No. 65 of 1828 and 1829.

(Signed) F. F. Clementson,
Deputy Accountant-General.

Signed, by the authority of the Right Hon. the Governor in Council, R. Clive,
Chief Secretary to Government.

I do hereby certify that the within is a registered promissory note, and that interest has been paid for two hundred and ten months, or to the 1st August, 1828, as per register.

Examined, R. De Silva. Certified, 20th January, 1829,
F. F. Clementson, D.A.G.

Madras, 2nd October, 1829. Received in cash the twelve months' interest due on the 1st August last, rupees 39,246-6-4. *Vide* letter from Government, dated 2nd December, 1829.

BINNY AND Co., Attorneys.

Madras, 20th August, 1830. Received in cash the twelve months' interest due on the 1st August, M. rupees 39,236-6-4. *Vide* letter from Government, dated 25th August, 1830.

BINNY AND Co., Attorneys.

Madras, 23rd Sept. 1831. Received in cash, the twelve months' interest due on the 1st ultimo, M. rupees 39,236-6-4.

BINNY AND Co., Attorneys.

The money invested and secured by the Company's paper was originally lent by the late Rajah Veer Rajundur Wadeer, the Rajah's paternal uncle since deceased, to the Madras Government, and the original Government security granted, which was for star pagodas 186,840, as well as the first substituted and the renewed Government security last hereinbefore mentioned, were taken, as is not uncommon among the natives of India, in the name of the Rajah Veer Rajundur Wadeer's daughter.

This person, whose name was Dewa Ammajee, and who was usually called Ranee of Coorg, by courtesy, and also to distinguish her from another Dewa Ammajee, the sister of the Rajah more particularly mentioned, for whom she has been more than once mistaken by the officers of the British Government, died previous to the occupation of Coorg by the British troops, leaving neither child nor husband living.

The interest on the said original Government security for star pagodas 186,840, and afterwards on the Government security for Madras rupees 653,940, into which the pagodas had been changed, as well as on the said last-mentioned renewed Government security, was regularly paid by the Madras Government to Ling Rajunder Wadeer, late Rajah of

Coorg, the Rajah's deceased father, from the time of his succeeding the late Rajah Veer Rajundur Wadeer, his deceased brother and the Rajah's uncle, up to the time of his the said Ling Rajundur Wadeer's death; and from that time, when his Highness succeeded as Rajah of Coorg, up to the year 1832, such interest was regularly paid to him through his constituted attorneys, the respectable firm of Binny and Co., then and still carrying on business at Madras as merchants and agents.

In the month of September, 1833, the Rajah transmitted, as usual, the last-mentioned Government security for Madras rupees 653,940, to his said agents and attorneys, to receive, for and on his behalf, the interest which had accrued due and payable thereon since the then last periodical payment made to them by the Government.

Messrs. Binny and Co., in the usual course of business, handed this Government security into the Madras Government treasury, in order to obtain the interest due thereon, allowing it to remain there for some considerable time, nor was it returned to them until February, 1834, when it was sent with a letter written and addressed to them by the Deputy Accountant-General of Madras, dated the 8th of that month. That letter was as follows:—

No. 4010.

To Messrs. Binny and Co.

GENTLEMEN,—I am directed by the Accountant-General to return to you herewith a promissory note of the Government in favour of her Highness Dewa Ammajee, Ranee of Coorg, as described in the margin,[1] which accompanied your letter of the 13th September last, the usual communication from Government for payment to you of the interest due thereon (as stated in a letter to your address from this department, dated 13th December last), not having been received up to this date.

[1] 6 per cent. Pro. note, dated 1st Feb. 1811. No. 65 of 1828-29. M. rs. 653,940.

I am to beg that you will be pleased to acknowledge the receipt of the bond.

I have the honour to be, Gentlemen,

Your obedient servant,

(Signed) S. CRAWFORD,

Deputy Accountant-General.

Fort St. George, Accountant-General's Office,
8th February, 1834.

Messrs. Binny and Co. thereupon wrote and addressed a letter to the Rajah, as he has been since informed, dated the 10th February, 1834, enclosing a copy of the last-mentioned letter, and informing him that they would hold "your Highness's bond," meaning the Rajah, and the said last-mentioned security, until they should hear further from him. This letter, and the copy of the Deputy-Accountant's letter, were forwarded through the official channel of the Resident of Mysore, under cover of a letter addressed to that officer. The Resident, however, did not forward to the Rajah the letters intrusted to him, but, as his Highness has since learnt, sent them in that same month, accompanied by a letter written by himself, to H. S. Græme, Esq., another officer of Government at Madras. The Rajah has been informed that in such letter the Resident of Mysore offered his advice to the purport and effect, that it would be expedient, during *the then present state* (that of hostility) *of the relations of the Company's Government with Coorg, to suspend the payment of interest* on the first-mentioned Government security of the Rajah, and to desire Messrs. Binny and Co. to keep the last-mentioned Government security in deposit until further instructions from the Government. Whether or no the information received by the Rajah was correct, the fact is, that the Company's Government have not paid any interest since that time to him, or to any person on or in respect of either of such Government securities, nor have such Government paid the principal moneys thereby secured.

On the 22nd of July, 1834, the same year in which the Rajah surrendered himself and family to Colonel Fraser, the Chief Secretary to the Madras Government wrote a letter to Messrs. Binny and Co., to the purport and effect following, that is to say, requesting them, by the direction of the Governor in Council, to deposit with the Accountant-General the said Government security for rupees 653,940 , standing in the name of Dewan Ammajee, and informing them that the Government would, if required, guarantee them against the consequences of any claim which might be preferred against them for the recovery of that Government security.

In answer to that letter, Messrs. Binny and Co. wrote and sent a letter to the Chief Secretary, bearing date the 24th July 1834, which, after acknowledging the receipt of the last-mentioned letter, proceeded in these words :—

" On the 13th September last, we received, under cover of a letter from the Resident in Mysore, a letter from the late Rajah of Coorg (meaning his Highness), enclosing a Government promissory note, in the name of Dewa Ammajee, Ranee of Coorg, for 653,940 rupees, with a request that we should receive the interest due on it, as we had for many years past been in the habit of doing. This, we presume, is the note alluded to in the letter from Government, and which we beg to disclaim any desire to retain possession of, or unwillingness to comply with the wishes of Government in respect to it, more particularly if protected by their guarantee from any pecuniary responsibility consequent to our doing so. We at the same time beg leave to submit that we are doubtful how far, as agents, we can deliver up a Government promissory note received from a constituent, to any one else, unless under his order and authority, without committing a breach of faith. We trust, therefore, that under the peculiar circumstances of the case, we are not soliciting too much when we submit our request, that the authority of the late Rajah of Coorg for our delivering up the promissory note may be obtained, or, if that is not expedient, that the opinion of the Government law-officer on the point in question may be taken, and furnished to us for our guidance. In conclusion, we would beg that his Excellency the Right Honourable the Governor-General in Council may be assured that the only cause for our hesitation in complying with the request now conveyed to us, consists in our fear of compromising our duties as agents.

"We have the honour to be, &c.,

(Signed) "BINNY AND CO."

The Chief Secretary to the Madras Government again wrote to Messrs. Binny and Co., but not, as it would appear, until the 4th April, 1837, and then only to the purport and effect following, viz.: that the Government did not acknowledge the proprietary right of the ex-Rajah of Coorg, meaning his Highness, to the Government security standing in the name of the late Dewa Ammajee, the daughter of the Rajah Veer Rajundur Wadeer.

It did not appear from this communication what was the particular ground upon which the Company rested their denial of the Rajah's proprietary right to this Government security, after having since the year 1821, when his Highness succeeded his father as Rajah of Coorg, up to the year 1831, paid, as above mentioned, regularly to him, through his attorneys Messrs. Binny and Co., the interest from time to time accruing due and payable thereon. If, however, the Government by such letter intended to set up the right of Dewa Ammajee to this security, by reason of the same standing in her name, it may be observed in reply:—

1st. That it is the custom throughout India for Hindoos to make purchases of lands, and to take securities for moneys lent, in the names of children and other members of their families, which are known and familiarly described as "Benamee transactions"; and, unless the contrary be shown by evidence, they are treated as trusts for their own use and benefit, and not for the individual benefit of the person whose name may be used. 2ndly. That even if the Government security in question were to be considered and treated as having been given by the father to his daughter Dewa Ammajee, as and for a provision for her, that lady had died without leaving either husband or child even before the British troops had occupied Coorg, and the Rajah was by Hindoo law upon her death entitled as heir to succeed to the stock secured by this document, and to hold in his own individual right such stock, and the document or security representing the same.

No reason or ground has ever yet been assigned by the Government, for not resuming the payment of interest to the Rajah on the other Government security standing in his own individual name, on the cessation of hostilities, which interest the Resident of Mysore had advised should be suspended only during the intermediate period, which was the utmost that ought or could have been done by international law.

If, however, the Company's Government should set up any claim either to the principal or interest of that Government security, or to the principal or interest of the stock represented by the other Government security standing in the name of the late Dewa Ammajee, the following objections are confidently made to any such claim.—First, that neither one nor other of the two several portions of stock was seized (by an act demonstrating an intention to seize and confiscate for the purposes of the state) *flagrante et nondum cessante bello*, so as to make a *hostile seizure* according to the law of nations. But there are two strong and incontrovertible facts to show that no such seizure or confiscation was then intended to be made: first, that such stock was never appropriated as booty or prize, although the booty found in cash and other property in the palace at Coorg, to the amount of upwards of £30,000, was seized and divided as prize, in the usual manner, among the troops engaged; secondly, that the several portions of stock, or the value thereof, now still stand in the respective names of the Rajah and the late Dewa Ammajee in the books of the East India Company. That is to say, the sum of sicca rupees 203,900 now still stands in the individual name of his Highness, and the sum of Madras rupees 653,940 now still stands in the name of the late Dewa Ammajee; the Government thereby admitting their liability to pay the same respectively. These sums have been from time to time brought forward in the same names in the said books and accounts, as subsisting charges against the territorial revenues of the Company.

But it was impossible that the Bengal or Madras Government could have acted in any other manner, as representing the Government of a nation like Great Britain, which, in common with all civilized nations of the world, respects and observes the rules of international law, in regard to war and its consequences. By that law,[1] stock in the public funds is respected as a sacred deposit, kept under the guarantee of the national faith, and is, therefore, unaffected by a war declared against the sovereign or nation who may be the creditor. If, through policy, the payment of the interest of the debt due to the enemy should be suspended during the continuance of hostilities, when these cease, the right to the interest and to the principal revives.

The payment as heretofore of the interest due on the Government securities, or Company's paper, not having been resumed after the cessation of hostilities, nor on the Rajah's reaching his final destination, he made several respectful applications to the Government on the subject, through the Government agent.

[1] "Everything that belongs to the nation is subject to reprisals, whenever it can be seized, *provided it be not a deposit intrusted to the public faith.* As it is only in consequence of that confidence which the proprietor has placed in our good faith that we happen to have such deposit in our hands, it ought to be respected, even in case of open war. Such is the conduct observed in France, England, and elsewhere, with respect to the money which foreigners have *placed in the public funds.*"—*Vattel's Law of Nations*, book ii. ch. 18, sec. 344.

"The state does not so much as touch the *sums which it owes to the enemy.* Money lent to the public is everywhere exempt from confiscation and seizure in case of war." —*Ibid.*, book iii. ch. 5, sec. 77, p. 323; and see also *Emerigon*, vol. i. p. 567; *Marten's Law of Nations*, 277.

To the first application only did he receive any answer, and then he was merely informed verbally that the Government did not recognise his claim. The last application made was in the year 1847, in a statement submitted, at his instance, by the Governor-General's agent to the Supreme Government of India, with the like result as before. His position as a state prisoner forbade the taking of any further steps to press home the justice of his claims. Those claims the Supreme Government never actually denied: his applications as mentioned were only passed over in silence; the fact being, that in the financial books of the East India Company the securities appèar in his own name.—

Nothing could exceed the attentions paid by the East India Company to the Rajah, on his arrival in the metropolis. He was invited to their sumptuous banquets, and many of the Directors felt honoured by introducing him to their private circle, and by being considered as his friends.

The Rajah's first care was to concert measures for accomplishing the chief object which had brought him to the British shores—the baptism, and subsequent English education, of his beloved daughter. After anxious and mature deliberation, he determined upon making known his wishes to her most gracious Majesty, in writing, in the hope of interesting that illustrious lady on behalf of his child; and the letter which he addressed to the Queen was as follows:—

Translation of a Letter to her Most Gracious Majesty the Queen, from his Highness the Rajah of Coorg.

(After compliments). 17th May, 1852.

I have most respectfully to represent to your Majesty, that my ancestors, after much and sincere endeavour, procured the friendship of the British Government. I also followed their example, and most eagerly continued that friendship.

My present object is respectfully to submit, that if your Majesty would be pleased to condescend to take my daughter under your gracious protection and kindness, in a manner becoming her position as a princess, it is my sincere and earnest wish to have her brought up in the principles of the Christian faith, as well as to give her an English education.

Before leaving India, I intimated this my desire to the Local Supreme Government, and two or three years after, to my great joy, I received permission to come to this country, whither, after a long and fatiguing journey, I have arrived with my young daughter.

As permission was granted me to come to this country, so I humbly hope that your Majesty will condescend to take my daughter under your Majesty's gracious protection; and, after having her baptized, your Majesty will be graciously pleased to cause her to be brought up and educated in the same manner as the daughters of the noblemen of this country, and instructed to follow the right path. This is my earnest desire; for I am convinced of the great good principles of your most gracious Majesty.

I may be permitted respectfully to observe, that up to this day no Rajah or Prince of India ever had conception of such a design. I took the first step towards it, and came here. This my object is worthy of your Majesty's support and assistance in every way, especially as I have no one here of my own countrymen. I, therefore, solely rely on the gracious kindness and generosity of your Majesty. When your Majesty, for the sake of your gracious name, will condescend to protect my child, she will then be happy and comfortable indeed, in every way. This is a great act of charity and benevolence, and it is well worthy of the countenance and support of sovereigns. For one may do such an act of kindness towards one's own, but to extend that benevolence to strangers, will be truly worthy of your most gracious Majesty.

With the exception of your Majesty, no one else is able to do this. Should this my object prove unsuccessful, I shall be put to shame before all India. It is in your Majesty's hands, therefore, to protect my character in this matter. By the mercy of the Almighty, I have hitherto passed my life in the true faith; this will be proved by my present intention. Although self-praise is inconsistent, yet one is sometimes forced to it. These few words, which I have respectfully submitted, will be fully comprehended by your Majesty. For the Almighty has given your Majesty a knowledge of all these things, and has placed you over a great nation. What shall I say more on this subject? I humbly solicit the favour of a reply to this my representation; after which, on some auspicious day, arrangements will be made for baptizing my daughter, when your Majesty's infinite kindness and condescension will become renowned. I am unacquainted with the English language, and have, therefore, caused a translation of this letter to be made in English, which is herewith forwarded.

May the Almighty bless your Majesty with health and happiness!—What more shall I say?

It was with the utmost satisfaction that the Rajah received, in reply, the following letter from the Right Honourable J. C. Herries, M.P., President of the Board of Control:—

India Board, 7th June, 1852.

Mr. Herries is commanded by the Queen to inform his Highness the Prince Veer Rajundur Wadeer that her Majesty has received his letter of the 17th May.

Her Majesty has commanded Mr. Herries to explain to the Prince Veer Rajundur Wadeer that it would not be in accordance with the usages of this country that her Majesty should take the charge of his daughter in the manner proposed by him. But her Majesty, being desirous of countenancing and assisting the praiseworthy intention of the Prince Veer Rajundur Wadeer to promote the instruction of his daughter in the principles of Christianity, and to constitute her a member of the Church of England, will confer with the Archbishop of

Canterbury on the subject, and will appoint a time, under his Grace's advice, for the performance of the ceremony of baptism, at which her Majesty is graciously pleased to signify her intention of being present, and of standing sponsor to the young princess.

Thinking that it would be but a mark of respect to make his Grace the Archbishop of Canterbury acquainted with his views respecting his daughter, the Rajah did himself the honour of writing to that right reverend prelate, as follows :—

Letter addressed to his Grace the Archbishop of Canterbury, by his Highness the Rajah of Coorg.

17th June, 1852.

MY LORD ARCHBISHOP,—My principal object for coming to this country, after an arduous and expensive journey, is to place my beloved daughter under the care and protection of her most gracious Majesty. If her Majesty will be graciously pleased to receive my child under her Majesty's protection, and support her as becoming her position in life, I am willing that my daughter should be educated in the principles of Christianity, and constituted a member of the Church of England. My only anxiety in this matter is, that my daughter be brought up as becoming her birth, so that I may not experience any humiliation when I return to my native country. It is an act worthy of her Majesty's gracious consideration, and I therefore trust and hope that your grace will also countenance and assist me to carry out my intention.

As your Grace kindly assured me, this morning, that I shall not experience disappointment with regard to my object in view, I entirely trust and rely on your Grace's kind assurance.

To the above letter his Grace the Archbishop was pleased to send a reply as under :—

Lambeth, June 19, 1852.

SIR,—I greatly approve your Highness's intention of bringing up your beloved daughter in the principles of the Christian religion. You thus do all that is in your power to promote her present and her eternal welfare. With this object in view, if it be your Highness's pleasure to leave the princess in this country, and to make provision for her education here, I shall be ready, if required, to give my advice concerning the person to whose care she may be properly intrusted, and to lend my assistance towards the accomplishment of the object you have at heart; in which I fervently hope, as I have before said, that your Highness may not be disappointed.

I have, &c. (Signed) J.

In reply to the letter addressed to him by command of her Majesty, and dated the 7th of June, the Rajah wrote as follows:—

Translation of a Letter from his Highness Veer Rajundur Wadeer, Rajah of Coorgh, dated 18*th June*, 1852.

To Her Most Gracious Majesty Queen Victoria.

MAY IT PLEASE YOUR MAJESTY,—The letter which your Majesty was graciously pleased to order to be addressed to me, under date the 7th June, 1852, I duly received, and the great gratification I experienced on my reading it cannot be expressed. In my first letter to your Majesty I endeavoured to explain my desires concerning my little daughter, in the best way I could according to my custom, that in whatsoever manner it may please your Majesty to dispose of my daughter, your Majesty shall ever receive the honour and respect due to so generous an action. I now further beg to pray that your Majesty will be graciously pleased to inform me of the day and hour on which I may come and make over my little daughter to your Majesty's protection, because if my daughter remain with me, she will not become acquainted with the manners and customs of this country, or the principles of the Christian faith. It would be, therefore, no advantage to her to remain with me, and it is for this reason that I desire to give her up to your Majesty's entire care and protection; and I humbly trust that your Majesty will be graciously pleased to accede to my request, so that when she is admitted into the Christian faith she may have no further need of my care, but remain entirely under your Majesty's august protection, and I shall feel tranquil. These my intentions I have ventured to address to your Majesty; for my daughter is also very anxious to live under the shadow of your Majesty's kind and gracious protection. After considering this, I humbly hope your Majesty will be graciously pleased to condescend to send me a reply; and if, as it is probable, I have failed in explaining my wishes clearly in this letter, I trust your Majesty will be pleased to send for me, that I may explain myself more fully in your Majesty's august presence, and I humbly submit that this would be the better way. May God bless your Majesty, and long may your Majesty reign in peace and security!

A few days afterwards the Rajah was gratified by receiving the following invitation:—

To His Highness Prince Veer Rajundur Wadeer.

The Lord Chamberlain is commanded by her Majesty to invite his Highness the Prince Veer Rajundur Wadeer to attend the christening of his daughter in the chapel at Buckingham Palace on Wednesday next, the 30th instant, at a quarter before one o'cleck.

June 28, 1852.

The ceremony took place accordingly at one o'clock in the afternoon of Wednesday, the 30th of June, 1852, in the private chapel of Buckingham Palace. The ceremony was performed by the Archbishop of Canterbury, assisted by the Rev. Lord Wriothesley Russell, Deputy Clerk of the Closet in Waiting, and the Hon. and Rev. Gerald Wellesley, Domestic Chaplain to her Majesty. Her Majesty the Queen was pleased to stand sponsor. The other sponsors were, the Viscountess Hardinge, Mrs. Drummond, and Sir James Weir Hogg, Bart., Chairman of the East India Company. The Princess was named by her Majesty "Victoria." Prince Albert, the Prince of Wales, the Princess Royal, Prince Alfred, and the Princess Alice, and Prince Veer Rajundur, were present at the ceremony. Her Majesty was attended by the Duchess of Atholl, Mistress of the Robes; the Viscountess Canning, Lady in Waiting; Lady Caroline Barrington, the Hon. Caroline Cavendish, and the the Hon. Flora Mocdonald, Maids of Honour in Waiting; the Marquis of Exeter, Lord Chamberlain; Lord Byron, Lord in Waiting; Colonel the Hon. C. B. Phipps; Sir Frederick Stovin, Groom in Waiting; Major-General Buckley, Equerry in Waiting; and Lieut.-Colonel Biddulph, Master of the Household. The Marquis of Abercorn, Groom of the Stole, and Colonel Bouverie, Equerry in Waiting, were in attendance on the Prince. The Viscount Hardinge; the Right Hon. John C. Herries, President of the Board of Control for the Affairs of India; and Major Drummond, 3rd Bengal Light Cavalry, were also honoured with invitations to attend the ceremony. After the christening the distinguished circle were conducted to the dinner-room, where luncheon was served. Prince Veer Rajundur and the Princess Gouramma, attended by their suite, left the Palace at twenty minutes past two o'clock.—

When the Rajah first arrived in this country, in March, 1852, the East India Company agreed to allow him, for his current expenses, the monthly sum of £100, to be deducted from the original pension of £6000; but on the 20th of May, 1853, the Court of Directors notified to him that no further remittance of his stipend would be transmitted to him after the 20th of March; and this they did upon the ground that the leave of absence had been granted with the understanding that his Highness was to return to Benares after the expiration of twelve months. No such condition, however, had ever been entered into by the Rajah, the only one imposed upon him by the Local Government having been that he should defray his own expenses.

In vain did the Rajah urge the unsatisfactory state of his health, and the consequent danger he should incur by being compelled to return to India; the interest he naturally felt in his daughter's welfare, &c.; his anxiety to witness her suitable establishment in life; and, lastly, his wish to await the decision of the High Court of Chancery, upon the suit which he had instituted against the Honourable Company. The Court of Directors still persisted in refusing to resume the payment of his pension, making his immediate return to India the *sine qua non* of their doing so.

It was under these circumstances that, in the hope of attracting the attention of the public to the Rajah's case, and engaging their sympathies in his behalf, the following summary of it was inserted in the *Daily News* of November 18, 1856:—

A PRINCE DETHRONED BY THE EAST INDIA COMPANY.

TO THE EDITOR OF THE DAILY NEWS.

SIR,—Permit me to occupy a little of your valuable space, by calling your readers' attention to the proceedings of the Honourable East India Company. I have been given to understand that the actions of that body in many instances are somewhat illiberal, but I would submit that in my own case they are particularly so; and certainly not in accordance with my own ideas of justice.

I am by birth and descent the rightful Rajah of Coorg, a mountainous principality in the south-west of India, and for thirteen years previously to the 24th April, 1834, I was an independent Hindoo prince and sovereign in alliance with the Honourable East India Company's Government, and as such was almost universally loved, respected, and even reverenced by my subjects.

My ancestors were of vast service to the Company, in fact, my late uncle rendered them such assistance in the year 1799, that they were enabled to cope with and finally completely overthrow the famed Tippoo Sultan, with whom the Company were at war, almost without intermission, from the year 1782 to 1799. That prince was master of all the coast provinces lying between the western mountains and the sea, and possessed all the intervening country from thence to the Carnatic, one solitary spot only excepted. That spot was the principality of Coorg; and while the Rajah, my uncle, denied the British troops entrance and exit, Tippoo Sultan's dominions were impregnable; but when the Company entered into a treaty with the Rajah of Coorg, he allowed the Bombay army under the command of General Abercrombie to pass through Coorg, forming a junction with the army of Lord Cornwallis, who, thus timely and powerfully reinforced, completely defeated Tippoo Sultan, and dictated a peace under the walls of Seringapatam, by which he ceded half his dominions unconditionally to the Company.

In consequence of this the Company entered into a treaty with the Rajah and his heirs for ever; which said treaty was to the effect that the Coorg territory should receive from the East India Company whatever assistance was needed, and in fact expressing the warmest and most enduring friendship for my uncle the Rajah and his successors. I myself have rendered the Company services on numerous occasions, and have received testimonials from them of a most flattering nature; but during the last few years of my reign their behaviour towards me materially changed; and eventually led to my dethronement and banishment.

In the year 1830, Chen Buswah (then one of my subjects) married my sister, Dewa Ammajee (although much against my wishes, and she was his second wife from our family, the first having died). In consequence of his being connected with royal blood, I provided for him from my own private purse in a manner becoming his station in life, and installed him in a suitable mansion a short distance from my capital. Things went on very well for some short time, but eventually it would appear that he became dissatisfied with his (supposed) subordinate position, and impatient of control; in consequence of which he, one night, drugged two of the officers in attendance upon him, bound one, hand and foot, and suspended him from the rafters of the house, where he was found dead in the morning; after which, Chen Buswah made off with his wife towards the Mysore country.

By stratagem he managed to pass a great distance unmolested, until he reached the barrier between my country and Mysore; on arriving there, however, he met with opposition, as the officer in command, suspecting something wrong, attempted to detain him. He was immediately shot dead by Chen Buswah, and another officer, who offered resistance, met with a similar untimely fate.

When these facts were communicated to me I immediately sent a formal demand to the Honourable East India Company (to whose territory he had fled) to surrender Chen Buswah as a prisoner, to be tried for the murders he had committed; to which they replied that they could not deliver up a party who had fled to them for protection. I afterwards, on several occasions, made similar requests, but with the same ill success.

This preyed on my mind exceedingly, particularly as the outrages committed by Chen Buswah were frequently commented on by my subjects; and therefore, instead of my anger being appeased by frequent allusions to this circumstance, it was constantly aroused, particularly as all my attempts were futile.

Some months after this event, a party arrived at Coorg, alleging that he came from Malabar for the purpose of seeing Mr. Græme (a member of the Madras Government); but, as he had no credentials, I thought it probable he was a spy, and ordered him to be detained as a hostage to compel the

Company to do me justice by delivering up Chen Buswah; and I was assured by those around me that this step would be the means of effectually accomplishing the object. To my surprise, however, the Company merely sent a formal demand for their messenger (as he afterwards in reality turned out to be), which, not being complied with, was followed by another. This I likewise considered I was not bound to obey. In consequence I was declared to be no longer an ally of the Honourable East India Company, and informed that my territories were annexed to the British possessions. Without any further notice an army was despatched against me, and troops entered my country at five different points. Finding myself in actual hostile collision with the British Government (whom I had been taught to consider from a child as my friends and protectors), I ordered flags of truce to be despatched, and surrendered myself. This was done for the purpose of saving bloodshed, as the onslaught would otherwise have been terrible. The Coorgs had congregated in an immense body, and were all armed to the teeth, prepared to do the most deadly execution. My palace was searched by the troops, and the valuables taken therefrom to the extent of £30,000, and the proceeds divided among the soldiery as prize-money.

Thus I became a state prisoner, and was hurried out of a country which had given me birth, amidst the lamentations of thousands of my subjects, who hovered around my *cortège*, weeping and bemoaning my hapless fate. Such expressions you will easily conceive, sir, however gratifying to the recollection now, then only served to render my position less endurable. In addition to this mark of respect from the poorer classes of my subjects, some hundreds of the nobility signed a memorial (which was thrust into my hand while I was being hurried away) expressing the most heartfelt sorrow at my departure, and concluding with a hope that my exile would be but temporary, and that I should return to my subjects again as their King, with renewed honour, and such expressions of kindness which made my heart, already filled with grief, ready to burst with feelings such as no words can express.

For fourteen years I was a prisoner at Benares, separated from all that was most dear to me. Permission was ultimately given to me by the Company for leave of absence for twelve months; and I came to England for the purpose of obtaining some permanent provision for myself and infant daughter, and to prosecute my claims against the Company, which consist in my being entitled to £180,000 sterling, the amount of bonds or promissory notes which I hold of theirs, and which said amount (in rupees) was absolutely paid and advanced by my ancestors and myself as a loan at a stipulated interest. The said interest, however, the Company have refused to pay since the year 1834. But this is not all. As my leave of absence expired in March last, and I did not think it advisable to return until some decisive step had been taken, I applied to the Directors for a prolongation of my leave, and in reply I received not only a positive refusal, but was informed, in conclusion, that my pension would not be continued, actually leaving me without any pecuniary resources whatever.

To make the already overflowing cup of bitterness more galling, I am described in Thornton's *History of British India* as tyrannical, haughty, and everything that a prince or ruler ought not to be, and in fact that my whole life was one of vice and infamy; but from the foregoing you will easily perceive that such is false, and the historian, in chronicling these words, must certainly have endeavoured to dish up details relative to myself in such a manner as to please the parties for whom his work was written—not knowing or thinking that the party on whom he had lavished so many disgraceful epithets would ever be in this country to confront him, and not only to deny the truth of the statement, but to be willing, ready, and able to prove, that there is no foundation for that which he has written.

The same writer has stated that the inhabitants of Coorg wished to become subjects of the Honourable East India Company; but this is not true either. That they submitted I will admit; but wherefore? They had lost their own sovereign, and as the weaker party, and without a leader to direct them, were forced to give into the stronger, let their feelings be what they might. The above observations will doubtless convince your readers that everything has been done to trample upon my feelings during my exile, and to paint me as an object unworthy the consideration or sympathy of an Englishman; but I am here, Mr. Editor, with a conscience guiltless of any crime or offence even, other than as above expressed and explained. I cannot conceive I have in any way infringed upon the Company's rights, or broken the treaty which my ancestors made with them. But I will pass this over: my kingdom has been taken from me, and I am an exile. I require only that which I am in every respect entitled to by the law of this land, by the law of nations and justice. I humbly but heartily appeal to the British public, through the medium of your valuable columns, to assist me in promoting my claims; and, from the hospitality I have already received, I feel sure that my entreaties will not be in vain.

In conclusion, it may not be irrelevant to mention that I have received the utmost kindness and condescension from her most gracious Majesty Queen Victoria, to whose care I with the utmost reliance commend my daughter. That amiable Queen stood sponsor to my child at her baptism, which was solemnized ten months ago; and at my wish and request she is being brought up in the Christian faith, which will, I hope, arm her with fortitude and resignation, and render her fitted for that life which is to come. I doubt not she will realize a fond father's most sanguine hopes and expectations; and in following the example of so excellent a Queen, she will be fitted for a happier and a better world.

My gratitude to the English nation as a body can but cease

with my life; and even then I shall perchance leave one behind who will live to show her own sentiments when my ashes rest in peace. She will then vindicate my past actions, and no doubt will convince Englishmen that my faults were not of the heart, and that a too confiding nature only had been the cause of my ruin, dethronement, and exile.

I have the honour to remain, sir, your obedient humble servant, VEER RAJINDER WUDAIR,

Once Rajah of Coorg.

23, Onslow-square, Brompton, Nov. 17, 1853.

The reader has already been informed of the kind manner in which the Marquis Dalhousie responded to the Rajah's request for permission to proceed with his daughter to England. Upon learning, therefore, that his lordship had returned to his native land, his Highness considered that he should be wanting in respect and gratitude, if he did not take an early opportunity of congratulating his lordship upon his arrival, and with this view he forwarded to the noble marquis a letter, a copy of which is as follows:—

20, Clifton Villas, Warwick-road, Paddington,
May 22, 1856.

MY LORD,—I take the earliest opportunity of most respectfully offering to your lordship my hearty and unfeigned congratulations, not only upon your safe arrival in your fatherland, but also upon your brilliant and successful career in the vast peninsula of Hindostan—a career which, for the benefits it has conferred upon the British empire in general, and upon India in particular, may rival the renowned administration of a Clive or a Wellesley.

Great, indeed, as is at all times the honour of being appointed to wield the vice-regal sceptre over dominions so extensive, and to sway the destinies of hundreds of millions of human beings, it is, in your lordship's case, still further enhanced by the consideration of that high and responsible charge having been wholly unsolicited, upon your part, and conferred upon you from the sole conviction that your lordship would prove to be—the right man in the right place.

Permit me, my lord, to say that while, in common with my countrymen, I admire and appreciate, and am thankful for the great and solid improvements which, under your lordship's auspices, have been effected throughout India, I feel personally indebted to your lordship for having permitted me, like other Indian princes and chiefs, to visit this country of power and civilization, in which I hope to have acquired no inconsiderable knowledge and information. Great, however, as is this my obligation to your lordship, it is but trifling when compared with what I owe you for the high distinction you have procured me in this world, and for those prospects which extend so infinitely beyond it; inasmuch as, but for you her most gracious Majesty Queen Victoria would not have done me the distinguished honour of standing sponsor to my beloved daughter the Princess Gouramma, nor would the latter have become, through the solemn rite of baptism, a member of Christ's pure and holy Church.

My lord, I shall not attempt to express by words the feelings of a heart over-fraught with gratitude; all I can say is, I *thank* you, and shall ever consider you as the best of benefactors.

Would to God that these congratulations and assurances were unalloyed, and that they could be addressed to one in the full enjoyment of that first of blessings—health! I trust, however, that severely as your lordship may be afflicted (the effect, no doubt, of our Indian climate and of incessant application to onerous duties), a return to your native country may, by removing the causes of your indisposition, restore to you all your wonted vigour.

Fearful of trespassing too long upon your lordship's attention, I shall now conclude with the humble but earnest request, that, so soon as your lordship is sufficiently recovered, I may be allowed the honour of paying my respects and thanks to you in a personal interview—an interview which will be but the renewal of an acquaintance that commenced in 1849. It will, doubtless, be in your lordship's recollection, that in the above year, when your lordship was on your way from the north-western provinces to Calcutta, myself and daughter had the honour of dining with your lordship at the house of Colonel Macgregor, at Benares, and I beg to assure your lordship that your kindness and affability to me upon that occasion will never be obliterated from my mind.

With sentiments of the most devoted respect, I have the honour to remain, your lordship's most obedient humble servant,

VEER RAJUNDUR WADEER, late Rajah of Coorg.

To the Rt. Hon. Earl Dalhousie, K.T., P.C., M.A., &c. &c.

His lordship replied as follows:—

Lord Dalhousie presents his compliments to his Highness Veer Rajundur Wadeer, late Rajah of Coorg, &c., in reply to the letter which he has received, dated 22nd May; he begs to state that he declines the interview which the Rajah requests.

Lord Dalhousie further begs to add, that, in the event of their meeting elsewhere, he must decline to recognise any acquaintance with the late Rajah of Coorg.

Brighton, June 2, 1856.

It was impossible for the Rajah to pass over, without observation, so gratuitous and unfeeling an affront as that contained in the above note; accordingly, on the 9th of June, he thus addressed his lordship by letter:—

Clifton Villas, June 9, 1856.

MY LORD,—I have received your lordship's letter, in reply to mine of the 2nd instant, and should have passed it over in silence, but for the concluding paragraph, in which your lordship is pleased to observe—"Lord Dalhousie further begs to add, that, in the event of their meeting elsewhere, he must decline to recognise any acquaintance with the late Rajah of Coorg."

Being wholly unconscious of having ever given to your lordship the slightest cause of personal offence, I can only attribute your lordship's unfortunate impression against me, to the malicious and slanderous reports so industriously propagated by my enemies; but I humbly conceive that, before acting upon those reports, your lordship's sense of justice and love of fair play should, at least, have given me an opportunity of disproving them, which, I rejoice to say, I can do, most fully and triumphantly.

Not content, however, with refusing to grant me the honour of an interview, your lordship has thought it not unbecoming your rank and character, to convey that refusal in terms as discourteous as they are unmerited on my part, and thus to aim an additional shaft at the victim of injustice and oppression.

As your lordship may readily conceive, I have found, by melancholy experience, how little sympathy attends misfortune; but it appears I had yet to learn that *mine* could ever have been considered, by one of your lordship's exalted station, as a butt for unprovoked, unfeeling, and deliberate insult.

I have the honour to remain your lordship's obedient servant,

VEER RAJUNDIR WAIDAAR, Rajah of Coorg.

Earl of Dalhousie, K.T., P.C., M.A., &c. &c.

Severe illness preventing the Rajah from accepting a card of invitation which had been sent him, for the ceremony of laying the first stone of "The Strangers' Home" Institution, his Highness addressed the following letter to the honorary secretaries of the society:—

20, Clifton Villas, Warwick Road, Maida Hill West,
May 31, 1856.

GENTLEMEN,—Permit me to tender you my cordial thanks for your polite invitation to be present at the interesting ceremony of laying the foundation-stone of the "Strangers' Home," &c., at the same time to express my sincere regret that ill health compels me to decline it. I assure you I greatly admire and fully appreciate the benevolent feelings that have prompted the erection and endowment of such a building as the one described in your prospectus, which has been read and translated to me by a friend.

Gentlemen, it is my opinion that, while it is the duty of all persons to whatsoever faith they may belong, whether they be Christians, Mussulmans, or Hindoos, to give a helping hand to this "labour of love," it is more especially incumbent upon those who have amassed riches in the sunny clime of India, to come forward in no niggard spirit upon the present occasion. Now, as far as my own countrymen are concerned, I am fully confident, that were the editors of the different English and vernacular newspapers, at present circulating in India, requested to notify gratuitously to their readers the objects and requirements of this proposed institution, and were the magistrates and other public functionaries to make known the same to opulent Indians, such as rajahs, princes, zemindars, nabobs, mahajuns, &c., a sum would be raised amply sufficient to carry out the objects of the society on a far more extensive scale than is even now proposed.

It is also in the power of the Local Government to further your views most efficiently, by making general, throughout the Presidencies, the regulations now in force at Bombay, by which all persons taking natives to England, in the capacity of servants, are required to give security for their being sent back to India when their services are no longer required. Convinced, as I am, gentlemen, of the immense good, both moral and physical, which will be effected by the institution, to inaugurate which you are now assembled, I the more deeply deplore that, owing to the peculiarly painful circumstances in which I am placed, in consequence of the denial of my just claims by a powerful corporation, I am precluded from contributing to your funds in the degree becoming my rank, or commensurate with my wishes for the success of the "Strangers' Home." My mite, however, such as it is, I cheerfully bestow, and hope that on some future, and perhaps not very distant day, when the dark cloud which now hangs over me shall cease so to do, I may be enabled to convince you that—"*Non ignarus mali, miseris succurrere disco.*"

I have the honour, gentlemen, to hand you £5, and remain your most obedient servant,

VEER RAJUNDER WADAIR, Rajah of Coorg.

To Lt.-Col. R. Marsh Hughes, and Major Tudor Lavie,
Hon. Secretaries to the "Strangers' Home."

The *Morning Post*, in giving insertion to the above letter, made the following observations :—

THE RAJAH OF COORG.

"We have much pleasure in inserting elsewhere the copy of a letter addressed to the president and directors of "The Strangers' Home" Society, by his Highness the Rajah of Coorg.

"Prevented by severe illness from being present in person upon that occasion, the Rajah availed himself of the opportunity to express, in graceful and feeling terms, his admiration of so excellent an institution, and, at the same time, his regret that, owing to the *res angusta domi*, his contribution was not such as to enable it to be considered as the true exponent of his good wishes for the success of so useful and philanthropic a society.

"Charity and benevolence never appear so amiable as in those over whom 'impends misfortune's threatening cloud,' and who, forgetting their own sufferings, endeavour to alleviate the distresses of others; and we are, therefore, the more gratified by this manifestation of the unfortunate Rajah's kind-heartedness, inasmuch as it tends to remove any unfavourable representations which may have been propagated against him."

The Marquis of Dalhousie having in his minute of the 28th of February, 1856, taken, what appeared to the Rajah, to be an erroneous view of two incidents—the adoption of the Christian faith by the Maharajah Dulleep Singh, and the Christian baptism of his (the Rajah's) daughter, his Highness addressed the following letter to the editor of the *Morning Post*:—

CHRISTIANITY IN INDIA.

July 2nd, 1856.

SIR,—My attention has been called to a minute of the Marquis of Dalhousie, the ex-Governor-General of India, which was recently published by order of the House of Commons, and in which his lordship is pleased to say :—

"There are two incidents connected with the families of native princes which remarkably signalize the period we are now reviewing, though they may not be regarded as of political moment.

"The first is the adoption of the Christian faith by Maharajah Dulleep Singh, the last of the rulers of the Punjaub. The act was voluntary on the part of the boy, and, under the guidance of God's hand, was the result of his own uninfluenced convictions. * * *

"The other incident is of a similar nature : I refer to the Christian baptism of the daughter of the ex-Rajah of Coorg, under the special protection of her Majesty the Queen."

Sir, with respect to the former of these incidents, I think that the noble marquis is entirely wrong when, in terms more befitting a pious frequenter of Exeter Hall than an astute and philosophic statesman, he attributes to *uninfluenced convictions* that which was the mere result of education. The facts are these :—

In the year 1847, when Maharajah Dulleep Singh Bahadoor was only nine years of age, he was forcibly separated from his mother, the Maharanee Jindân Kour, the only relative he had left in the world, and transferred to the care of the British authorities, as appears from the following extract of a letter addressed by the Resident at Lahore to the Secretary of the Governor-General of India, and dated Lahore, Aug. 20, 1847:

"Sirdar Shere Singh asked me this morning, how the news should be broken to the young prince; and, as the sirdar said that, although a boy, the Maharajah had already begun to understand his mother's character, and the impropriety of sundry goings-on in the palace, I advised a plain, but kind, statement of the real truth, viz., that the Maharanee's reputation was so notorious, her vices so incorrigible, and her example so pernicious, that the Governor-General thought it wrong to leave him with her any longer. Word has just been brought that the Maharajah took this disclosure with much indifference, is deeply engaged in playing, and sent me his salaam"!!

So that, according to the noble marquis, here is a child only nine years old, and who, up to that time, had never, in all probability, heard the word—Christianity—pronounced, found suddenly embracing that faith from the mere impulse of *uninfluenced convictions*. What wonderful precocity surely the boy must have evinced!

> "In school divinity as able
> As he that hight irrefragable."

Did the noble marquis never read in the Koran, "that every child is born a Mahommedan, but that it rests with the parents to make him either a Jew or a Christian"?

None, perhaps, except the followers of the false prophet, will assent to the former of these assertions; but who is there, with a single grain of common sense in his composition, be he Christian, Jew, or Turk, that will object to the latter, or not admit—

> "'Tis education forms the infant mind,
> Just as the twig is bent the tree 's inclined."

As for myself, sir, although brought up in the Hindoo religion, I no sooner assumed the reigns of government than, utterly abhorring and detesting the worshipping of idols, I emancipated myself from its trammels; so much so, indeed, that during my twenty years' exile at Benares, I never once entered a pagoda or temple, averting even my eyes from them; while, to discourage superstition still further by my example, I never, during the eclipses of the sun or moon, bathed in the river Ganges—a rite considered so solemn by the Hindoos, that, in order to fulfil it, thousands of thousands perform a long and weary pilgrimage to the sacred city.

Not satisfied with having abjured a false religion, I should have proceeded still further and embraced Christianity myself, had I not feared that, by so doing, I should sow dissension and ill will among a large circle of dear relatives and friends. As it was, however, I have brought up one daughter in that faith; and had the East India Company, after deposing me, confiscating my revenues, and seizing my treasures, assigned me a more liberal allowance than they did, I might then have saved a sufficient sum to defray the expense of having *all* my children similarly educated.

I have the honour to be, sir, your most obedient servant,

VEER RAJUNDER WADDEER, Rajah of Coorg.

The Rajah finding that all his representations to, and expostulations with, the Hon. East India Company failed to induce them to render him justice, determined, at length, upon making an appeal to Parliament; and upon his forwarding a statement of his case to the Marquis of Clanricarde, that nobleman most generously undertook to introduce the subject before the House of Lords. The following is an accurate report of the discussion which took place on that occasion:—

THE RAJAH OF COORG.

The Marquis of CLANRICARDE called the attention of her Majesty's Government, and of their lordships, to the case of the

Rajah of Coorg. The Rajah of Coorg, it appeared, had formerly been one of their most loyal allies in British India, but in course of time his country became involved in war, and he was himself made prisoner. The Indian Government settled a pension upon him, and removed him from his own country to Benares, where he had lived for upwards of eighteen years, during which time he conducted himself with the loyalty of a good subject, and won the esteem of all who knew him. In 1850 he applied for leave to come to England for the purpose of superintending the education of his daughter, whom he wished to be brought up as a Christian. Leave was granted to him by the East India Company for one year. Now, every one knew that when the East India Company gave leave of absence to their servants, they did not limit it to one year. The Rajah represented that a year would be insufficient for his object; and he was formally informed that it was customary to give leave for one year, and that he could apply, if he required it, for an extension in England. He, accordingly, came to England in 1852, and in the spring of 1853, he renewed his application to be allowed to remain in England. His application was peremptorily refused; and because the East India Company had not the power to seize his person in this country (*hear, hear*), they determined to stop his pension, with the exception of that portion of it that was necessary for the support of his family. A more despotic act never was perpetrated. (*Hear, hear.*) The Rajah had been now, in all, two-and-twenty years a subject of England, and he had conducted himself in the most loyal and becoming manner; and the attempt to remove him from this country, he (the Marquis of Clanricarde) must say, was a most tyrannical act, for which no reason had been alleged. The only question was his desire to stay here. His health was precarious, and his medical advisers had told him that this country was more healthy for him than India; but the East India Company had sent their physician to examine him, and he said there would be no danger in his returning to India by a sea voyage at a certain season of the year; but he (the Marquis of Clanricarde) must repeat that the conduct of the Company was most tyrannical. And that was not all. Their lordships would hardly believe that the person so treated was at law with the East India Company, and was at that moment prosecuting a suit in Chancery against them for the recovery of property; and they, under such circumstances, exercised their power most tyrannically to get him out of the way, at the very time when his presence in this country was of the utmost importance. Was there one of their lordships who would not allow that that was an act of tyranny? and he was sure that it was an act which the Parliament of this country would not allow. (*Hear.*) It was impossible, however, that any British Minister could sanction the treatment of a prince in that manner; and he was sure that his right hon. friend (Mr. Vernon Smith) would not sanction it, and therefore he had only to ask the Government what were the grounds upon which the East India Company insisted on the return of this nobleman to India, or upon which, in default of such return, they claimed the right to withhold the amount they had contracted to give him while in this country.

The Duke of ARGYLE said, the noble marquis seemed better informed upon the details of the Rajah's case than he was, for he had not seen any of the papers, and was only acquainted with the general state of the facts. He believed that the Board of Control had no power whatever to compel the East India Company to pay the allowance which they had withheld from the Rajah. The noble marquis had stated the facts correctly, and by his statement he implied, that the Company had power to require the return to India of this prince, who was considered in that country to be a prisoner of war. He might say, in relation to the question, that the East India Company in this country exercised considerable power in reference to those under them; and with reference to the Rajah, he might say the fact was, this prince had been considered in India a prisoner of war, and when he asked for leave to come to England, it was granted for twelve months, but whether with the assurance that the period would be extended at its expiration he could not say. It was quite clear, that if the Rajah had been a private individual, no such leave would have been required; but the East India Company, from the nature of his position, having the right to grant or withhold it, the demand made upon him to return at the expiration of the leave, could hardly be stigmatized as a tyrannical or unjustifiable act. He (the Duke of Argyle) did not think it desirable that this prince should be allowed to remain in this country, expending the allowance given to him by the East India Company; and with regard to his being engaged in carrying on a lawsuit in the Court of Chancery against the East India Company, he (the Duke of Argyle) thought that he could carry it on quite as well by instructions to his lawyers. It was well known, that in cases of this kind, correspondence was frequently carried on in England by deposed Indian princes with their former subjects, and therefore it was necessary that the East India Company should act with caution.

The Earl of Ellenborough confirmed the accuracy of the noble duke's statement, that the Board of Control had no power whatever to compel the Court of Directors to pay the prince the sum they agreed to give him during the year he had leave of absence. The noble marquis had stated the facts of the case correctly, and he (the Earl of Ellenborough) must say that, taking into consideration all the circumctances, the conduct of the Court of Directors, in refusing payment to the prince, was very ungenerous and unwise (*hear, hear, hear*); but, at the same time, he agreed with the noble duke, that it was neither for the advantage of native princes, nor generally for the advantage of the Government of India, that those princes should come and reside in this country, in order to prosecute their claims. He had himself privately advised the Rajah of Coorg, four years ago, to return to his own country, being quite confident that it would be more to his own credit and comfort to rest in the midst of his family at Benares, where he was very much respected, than to reside as an individual unknown in this country. As to the suit against the East India Company for the recovery of his property, he could not comprehend how a question of that kind between two sovereigns—for such they were—could be made the subject of inquiry before the Court of Chancery; and he believed it would be found, in the course of the investigation, that the property neither belonged to the Court of Directors, nor the Government of India, nor the Rajah, but to the Crown, and that it had been misappropriated by the Government of India. If this prince were dispossessed of his property in consequence of military operations, it clearly, as the prize of war, belonged, not to the Government of India, but to the Crown; and if the Crown asserted its right, the Rajah would be deprived of all excuse for not returning, and the Company of any reason for conducting themselves towards him in a manner most ungenerous and uncourteous; under these circumstances he would suggest that the attention of the law officers of the Crown should be drawn to the subject.

It appearing to the Rajah, upon reading the Duke of Argyle's speech, that his Grace had been misinformed upon some points of his case, his Highness took the liberty of addressing the following letter to the noble Duke:—

20, Clifton Villas, July 22, 1856.

MY LORD DUKE,—The very great respect which I entertain for your Grace, as a member of the House of Peers, not less than as filling so distinguished a post in her Majesty's Government, would, I confess, under any other circumstances than those in which I am placed, have deterred me from taking so great a liberty as that of addressing to your Grace a few remarks upon what fell from your Grace's lips on Monday, 21st instant, in the House of Lords, upon the occasion of the Marquis of

Clanricarde's asking the Government a question respecting the treatment I have received from the East India Company. Your Grace is represented, in the report of the *Times* newspaper of the 22nd instant, as having said—

1. That I was considered in India as a prisoner of war.

2. That I had leave given me to come to England for one year.

3. That, at the expiration of that time, I was desired to return to India, and, although I asked permission to remain longer, yet, as it was competent for the East India Company to grant that request or not, their withholding the permission could not be considered an act of tyranny.

4. That the East India Company considered it objectionable that persons in my situation should continue in England, expending here the revenue granted them by the Company.

5. That your Grace could not think that there was any reason to impute to the East India Company a desire to impede me in the prosecution of my lawsuit, because I being in India could conduct that quite as well as if I were in England, through the means of legal agents.

6. That very considerable inconvenience was experienced by the local Government of India by the residence of individuals in my position in England, for they carried on a correspondence with their former subjects, inducing sometimes the belief that they would recover their power.

REMARKS.

1. It is perfectly true, I am considered as a prisoner of war, and have been so for twenty-two years: a length of detention, however, which might, I humbly conceive, have entitled me to the benefit of an act of amnesty, the more especially as, during the whole of that time, I have comported myself to the unqualified satisfaction of the Company's officers, under whose surveillance I was placed, as I can prove by their own letters, which are in my possession. This severity, not to say tyranny, on the part of the East India Company, becomes the more conspicuous when contrasted with the graceful clemency of her

Majesty, who granted her free pardon to convicted traitors (O'Brien and others), after a detention of eight years, being only about a third part of mine.

2. My leave of absence was not given me on the condition that I was to return at the expiration of twelve months, nor have the East India Company any evidence, written or parole, to prove that it was granted under such a proviso. I perfectly well remember that, upon that occasion, I asked the late Major Stewart, my superintendent, whether, if I chose to return home before the expiration of twelve months, or prolong my stay beyond that term, there would be any objection to my so doing. His reply was, "It is only a matter of form; we ourselves apply for one year's leave of absence, which, upon our application, is always extended, although some inconvenience may arise to the service therefrom; it is an understood thing."

3. I do not pretend to question the competency of the East India Company to deny my request, but, circumstanced as I am, their refusal renders them obnoxious to the charge, if not of tyranny, at least to that of harshness and undeserved severity. The East India Company were fully informed of the objects for which I came to England, viz., to superintend the education and progress of my daughter, and prosecute my claim against them: objects which they well knew could not be accomplished within so short a period as that of one year.

4. It appears singular that the objection of the East India Company to absenteeism should be suspended in the case of Maharajah Duleep Singh, an Indian prince residing in this country, and spending forty times more than is allotted to me; but, however this may be, the objection cannot possibly apply to me, for out of the annual allowance of £6000 made to me by the East India Company, £4320 is paid to my family at Benares, and is spent by them there, and £480 is assigned to my daughter's education and support in this country.

5. The fact of my being compelled to return to India would be fatal to my suit in Chancery —

a. By the loss of time incurred in communicating, even should I be allowed so to do, with my solicitors, from so great a distance.

b. By there not being any English solicitor or lawyer at Benares with whom I could consult.

c. By the order which, there is no doubt, would be sent to the British Resident at Benares, to prevent me from holding any correspondence with parties in England.

6. I have no right to call in question the assertion of the Honourable Company with respect to other persons similarly situated as myself; it may or may not be correct; but, for myself, I most solemnly and emphatically declare that I have never taken part in any intrigues of whatsoever nature against the Honourable Company, and that I have never held any correspondence with any person or persons in Coorg who were my former subjects. The favourable opinion of my conduct entertained and expressed by Lord Ellenborough as Governor-General, by Lieut.-Colonel Carpenter, Lieut.-Colonel M'Gregor, and others, who, from their official situation, were fully competent to form a correct opinion, sufficiently exonerates me from so unjust, because unfounded, an imputation.

Believe me, my Lord Duke, when I assure your Grace, it is no idle wish to controvert what your Grace has been pleased to advance, that has induced me to venture upon these remarks. Conscious that ever since my deposal I have never meditated, much less performed, any act prejudicial to the East India Company, or their interests, I feel more acutely their unjust treatment of me, and am the more anxious to vindicate myself. The consequences of my obeying their order, would be the exacerbation of my disease to a degree which would endanger my life itself, and the infallible destruction of my suit in Chancery, for the reasons above stated.

Apologizing to your Grace for thus encroaching upon your very valuable time, I remain, &c.

His Grace the Duke of Argyle, &c. &c.

The debate was resumed on the 25th of July, by the Marquis of Clanricarde, who said :—

My Lords, I now rise to move for copies of any minute of the East Indian Government in 1834, specifying the terms and conditions of the allowance to be made to the deposed Rajah of Coorg. The more I learn on the question of the tyranny practised upon this unfortunate prince, the more discreditable the conduct of the Indian Government appears. I hope that the members of the Government in this House will give us an assurance that Mr. Vernon Smith will inquire into this subject, and that the result will be, that the Rajah of Coorg will be allowed to reside in the capital of his sovereign, unless some good reason should be shown why he should not do so. As yet no reason whatever has been shown against it. I know it is said that it is inconvenient for these Indian princes to be coming over and spending their income in this country. But, my lords, I should like to ask to whom it is inconvenient? It cannot be inconvenient to any honest man. I cannot understand on what ground the East India Company require this prince to spend his money in India, particularly as his allowance from them is only £1200. I am astonished that they should have the audacity to talk of the inconvenience of spending Indian revenue in this country, when I hear of their paying £700 to one counsel, and £500 to another, for giving them bad advice.

My lords, the Rajah of Coorg is a man to whom the East India Company are under great obligations, and instead of allowing him £1200 a year, and refusing him permission to reside in this country, he ought to have received very different treatment at their hands.

A noble lord, the other night, expressed his astonishment at the affairs of an Indian prince getting into the Court of Chancery; but I say, "Thank God we have a Court of Chancery!" The East India Company refused this unfortunate prince the documents necessary to prove his claims, but they could not do that when the matter was carried into the Court of Chancery. My lords, the conclusion to which I cannot avoid coming is, that they want the Rajah to be forced out of this country, that he may not be able to attend to his lawsuit in Chancery, which he has instituted to enforce his rights.

My lords, so far from its being inconvenient that these Indian princes should come to reside in this country, I think nothing can be better calculated to educate and Christianize the natives of India, than that those of them who can afford it should come over here, to inform themselves as to the manners and customs, the literature and religion of this country. I believe that the voluntary return of native princes, like the Rajah of Coorg, to India, after they have lived for some years at the centre of British civilization, and near the Court of their Sovereign, is more calculated to benefit India, and consolidate British power in that country, than any attempts, dictated by a miserable jealousy, to send those princes back to their native country. I venture to say, my lords, that there never was an instance yet, in the history of nations, of a chief who, being conquered, was driven from the capital of the conquering country, against which he had no inclination to intrigue, and of which he had become the subject. I do hope that the Government will not object to this return, and that they will take the case of this prince into their consideration. (*Hear, hear.*)

The Duke of ARGYLE.—I explained the other night that I did not feel called upon, on behalf of the Government, to defend the course taken by the East India Company on this subject. They do not feel called upon to express an opinion either for or against it, because it does so happen that the law for the payment of pensions does give a very large discretion on that point to the East India Company. It is not a matter in which the Government has full right to control the East India Company. If Parliament should think fit to alter the constitution of the Indian Government in that particular—if, at any future time, Parliament should think right to give the Government more power—then it would be a different question. But, hitherto, Parliament has exhibited considerable jealousy in giving the Home Government power of control directly over the revenues of India. Personally I may say, that I rather agree with the noble marquis, and that I do not see any harm in allowing this old prince to remain in London as long as he wishes to do so. (*Hear, hear.*) I believe, however, he was in such a position as to require leave of absence from India from the Company. I believe that, on condition of spending a year in this country, leave was given for one year, and, after the expiration of that period, the Company signified their wish to the Rajah of Coorg that he should return to India.

The Earl of Ellenborough.—I think the noble marquis had better alter the terms of his motion. The Company will say there is no minute, and one year will be lost. If "orders" are then substituted, they will say there are no orders, and another year will be lost. The noble marquis had better take general words, and then the Company cannot escape from making some return.

The Marquis of Clanricarde.—I am obliged to the noble earl, and will adopt his suggestion.

The motion was then amended, and, as amended, agreed to.

The following petition was also presented (July 28, 1856) to the House of Commons, by Mr. Milner Gibson:—

App. 1281. *Mr. Milner Gibson.* Sig. 1.

13,819. This petition of Veer Rajunder Waidar, late Rajah of Coorg,

Humbly showeth,—That your petitioner was an independent Hindoo Sovereign Prince until the year 1834, when he was conquered by the East India Company's forces, and sent a state prisoner to Benares.

2. That the East India Company took possession of your petitioner's dominions, seized his treasures and valuables, to the amount of £150,000 sterling, and, in flagrant violation of the law of nations, appropriated to themselves the capital of £80,000 East India Stock, together with the dividends thereon, which sum was held by your petitioner for moneys lent at various times to the said East India Company, by the uncle and father of your petitioner.

3. That, in the year 1852, your petitioner obtained leave of absence for one year from the Local Government, for the purpose of visiting England.

4. That, upon your petitioner's arrival in England, a monthly allowance of £100 was made to him by the East India Company.

5. That this monthly allowance was deducted from an annual one of 60,000 rupees, assigned by the East India Company to your petitioner upon his being deposed by them, the residue thereof being paid to your petitioner's family at Benares.

6. That, shortly after your petitioner's arrival in London, he instituted a suit in Chancery against the East India Company, for the recovery of the aforesaid £80,000 stock, your petitioner's claim to which the East India Company refused to recognize, notwithstanding that the said stock stands in your petitioner's name in the said Company's ledgers.

7. That, upon your petitioner's applying to the Local Government for leave to visit England, he distinctly stated that it was his intention so to institute the said suit.

8. That, after your petitioner had resided one year in England, the East India Company stopped his monthly allowance of £100, under the pretext that he had engaged to return to India after the expiration of twelve months, an assertion contrary to fact, and one which the said East India Company have no evidence, written or parole, to substantiate.

9. That the East India Company make your petitioner's

immediate return to India the *sine qua non* of their renewing the aforesaid monthly stipend of £100.

10. That three reasons prevent your petitioner's complying with this harsh and unjust condition :—

(*a.*) The very precarious state of his health, as proved by medical certificates.

(*b.*) His anxiety for the suitable establishment in life of his beloved daughter, whom he brought over to this country for the purpose of being educated in the Christian religion.

(*c.*) His wish to await the decision upon his case by the High Court of Chancery.

11. That the East India Company's object in thus peremptorily insisting upon your petitioner's return to his native country is that of crippling his resources should he attempt to remain in England, or, should he consent to go back to India, of obstructing the progress of his Chancery suit—1. By the loss of time incurred in communicating, even should he be allowed to do so, with his solicitors; 2. By there not being any English solicitor or lawyer at Benares with whom he could consult; 3. By the order which, there is no doubt, would be sent to the British Resident at Benares to prevent your petitioner from carrying on any correspondence with parties in England.

12. That ever since your petitioner's deposal, he has cautiously abstained from engaging in any intrigues against the East India Company; and that, since his arrival in England, he has never carried on any correspondence whatsoever with any person or persons in Coorg.

Your petitioner, therefore, most humbly but earnestly entreats that your honourable House, exerting the power with which it has been invested for defending the weak against the strong, and vindicating the cause of the oppressed, will procure your petitioner redress, by obtaining for him the continuance of his aforesaid pension of £100 per month, together with the payment of all arrears of the same which may now be due to him.

And your petitioner will ever pray, &c.

VEER RAJUNDER WAIDAR, late Rajah of Coorg.
20, Clifton Villas, Warwick Road, Maida Hill West,
July 23, 1856.

On August 4th the Rajah made his last appeal to the justice of the Hon. Company, by the following letter:—

To the Honourable the Court of Directors of the Honourable East India Company.

HONOURABLE SIRS,—I duly received the answer you were pleased to order should be returned to my last communication, and although my regret is necessarily great at learning therefrom, that you still adhere to your determination of withholding the payment of my monthly allowance, yet that regret is, in some degree, modified by the assurance, that "your refusal to pay me my pension, in this country, has no reference to the fact of my being engaged in litigation against the East India Company."

As I apprehend, therefore, the reason of that refusal is now confined to my declining to return forthwith to India; but I have yet to learn in what respect my remaining here a short time longer, can be injurious to the Company, more especially after the disclaimer you have made as above, touching my suit in Chancery.

As regards the state of my health, Dr. Lewis, my medical attendant, still adheres to his opinion, that until I am perfectly convalescent, the voyage to India would be most perilous for me.

With respect to my suit in Chancery, my removal to India would inevitably prove fatal to it, if only from the loss of time necessarily incurred in communicating with my legal advisers here, even should I be allowed to do so, which is extremely doubtful, as well as from the fact, that there is no English solicitor or attorney at Benares with whom I could consult.

As to my pension, allow me, Honourable Sirs, to observe, that had I insisted upon the whole of it (£6000) being paid to me in this country, you might then, indeed, have been justified, by circumstances, in your refusal to comply; but it is only a portion of that pension which I ask you to continue, in fact only one-fifth part thereof. What then, let me ask, can be your objection to my disbursing a sum comparatively so small, for a short time longer, in this country?

The same reason which induces you to withhold my pittance ought, surely, to operate equally in the case of his Highness the Maharajah Duleep Singh, and yet you permit that prince to expend the whole of his allowance, which is forty times * greater than mine, in this country, nor have you imposed any limitation to his stay therein.

But in what are his Highness's claims to your indulgence superior to mine?

Removed, when nine years old, from the Ranee, his mother, he received an English education, and was brought up in the Christian faith. Everywhere the object of attention and regard, and, I believe, deservedly so, on account of his amiable, unassuming, and prepossessing manners, he has been free from all those cares, anxieties, and afflictions, which have nearly bowed me to the grave; he has never known the humiliation of having been vanquished in the field, the mortification of having been despoiled of his treasures, and the irksomeness of a twenty years' detention. Young, he has yet in prospect many years of prosperity and happiness; whereas if I, suffer-

* Terms granted to the Maharajah Duleep Singh Bahadoor, on the part of the Hon. East India Company, 29th March, 1849, Art. 4, and ratified by Earl Dalhousie, Governor-General, 5th April, 1849: "His Highness Duleep Singh shall receive from the Hon. East India Company, for the support of himself, his relations, and the servants of the state, a pension not less than four, and not exceeding five lacs of Company's rupees per annum."—Return to an Order of the Hon. House of Commons, dated 23rd May, 1856. East India House, 7th July, 1856, p. 57.

ing at once with age and infirmities, venture to throw a glance upon the few years which Providence may still vouchsafe me, I can descry nought but gloom and wretchedness, unless you, Honourable Sirs, relent, and deign to shed over them a gleam of comfort and a ray of hope.

Had I, Honourable Sirs, taken any part in intrigues against your Honourable Company; had I assembled around me disaffected natives, and concocted with them schemes for annoying or injuring the East India Company; or had I held a secret correspondence with any of my former subjects in Coorg, for the purpose of endeavouring to recover my lost power—then, indeed, I should have merited, and you, Honourable Sirs, would have been justified in inflicting upon me, this act of undue severity; but even you, yourselves, Honourable Sirs, will fully acquit me of such conduct, holding, as I do, the testimonials of your own officers to the invariable propriety and correctness of my deportment.

Honourable Sirs, I feel confident that when you calmly consider my case, as individuals, apart from your corporate capacity, there is not one of you, who, laying his hand upon his breast, will say—I approve of depriving the old Rajah of Coorg of his monthly stipend—I approve of forcing this old man, who has never done me any wrong, to return to India at the peril of his life—I approve of separating him from his daughter, "the child of his bosom," that child whose spiritual welfare was one of the chief objects of his coming to this country—I approve of throwing insurmountable obstacles in his way of obtaining what he considers his just claims, by interposing oceans between him and his legal advisers.

Will you, then, Honourable Sirs, approve, collectively, that which you condemn, individually?

Honourable Sirs, your physical power is undoubtedly great, but it is not that alone which supports your vast empire: it is the moral influence you have there obtained, that is the surest bulwark of your dominion; and any act, however trifling and insignificant it may appear, which is calculated to diminish that influence, impairs your strength, and undermines your authority.

Reflect that it is not my case alone which has recently been brought before the British and, consequently, before the Indian public; and although an individual instance of injustice may pass unnoticed, repeated ones may lead to the most deplorable and fatal consequences.

I, therefore, Honourable Sirs, most humbly, but most earnestly entreat and implore you to reconsider my case, not only as the masters of a vast and powerful empire, but also as Christian men desirous of "doing unto others as you would yourselves be done unto," and as fellow-men, united to me by the sympathies of our common nature.

By the exercise of your power you can abridge the few remaining years still left me in this world. Will you do so?

By the exercise of your justice you can render the residue of my existence comfortable and happy. Will you do so?

I am, with the most profound respect, Honourable Sirs, your most obedient humble servant,

VEER RAJUNDER WAIDAR, late Rajah of Coorg.

20, Clifton Villas, Warwick Road, Maida Hill West,
London, August 4, 1856.

On the 13th of September, the Rajah had the satisfaction of receiving from the Hon. Court of Directors a reply, the copy of which is as follows:—

East India House, September 12, 1856.

SIR,—I am commanded by the Court of Directors of the East India Company to acknowledge the receipt of your letter of the 4th ultimo, and, in reply I am directed to inform you, that as you state your return to India at the present time would "inevitably prove fatal" to the lawsuit you have instituted against the East India Company, and as the Court of Directors are desirous that no obstacle should be opposed to the adjudication of the said suit, on its own merits, you are permitted to remain in England, until further communication with the Government of India, of which notice will be given you.

I am directed to add that your pension will be paid in full, by the Government of India, from the time of the suspension of its payment.—I have, &c.

(Signed) J. D. Dickinson, Assist. Secretary.

To H.H. Veer Rajunder Wadeer, Ex-Rajah of Coorg.

Desirous of not interrupting the thread of our narrative, we have hitherto refrained from noticing, with a view to refutation, the grave charges which, shortly before and after his deposal, were brought against the Rajah. We shall now proceed to offer a few observations upon them, premising, in the first place, that it is important to remark that no attempt has ever been made by the East India Company to establish the truth of these charges, either officially or by witnesses confronted with the accused in a court of justice; and that, until this be done, the Rajah must be considered innocent of them, by virtue of the well-known maxim of English law, that no man shall be considered guilty until proved to be so. Secondly, that accusations of this description are always justly liable to suspicion, when they are known to be made from interested motives; and such was the case, for the East India Company, being about to violate the law of nations by the dishonest confiscation of the Rajah's *funded property*, considered it necessary to palliate their injustice by blackening the character of their victim, and thus depriving him of all public sympathy. "Those princes," says Howitt, "that were once subjected to the British power or the British friendship, were set up or pulled down just as it suited the pleasure of their conquerors or their friends. If necessary, *the most odious stigmas* were fixed on them, to get rid of them; they were declared weak, dissolute, or illegitimate."[1]

Such indeed has been the Company's invariable rule in all similar cases. Is the annexation of an unoffending ally considered expedient?—is the transfer of the contents of his full coffers to their empty treasury deemed desirable?—is the extinction of a burdensome debt regarded as convenient?—the word is given that all calumnies against him will be thankfully received by the Resident, to be afterwards chronicled by mendacious historians, and propagated by hypocritical missionaries: the game is then started, and the unfortunate prince is hounded on to ruin, and perhaps to death.

Two most serious charges have been brought against the Rajah:—

1. That of having murdered his own sister and her children.
2. The perpetration of murder and oppression generally.

The circumstances under which the first of these charges was made were these:—The Rajah had forwarded, through the Court of Directors, to the Indian Government, a memorial, dated June 8, 1853, on the subject of the stock standing in the name of his sister the Princess Dewa-Ammajee, whose heir he was, and which stock amounted to 653,940 rupees, or £65,394 sterling. After a lapse of more than a year, his Highness received the following reply:—

Foreign Department, Fort William,
30th June, 1854.

Sir,—Your memorial, dated London, June 8, 1853, to the address of the Court of Directors, having been duly forwarded by that body to the Government of India, I have now the honour, by direction of the Most Noble the Governor-General in Council, to transmit to you the accompanying extract from a despatch just received in reply from the Hon. Court, containing their decision on your claim to certain Government

[1] *The English in India*, page 12.

promissory notes belonging to the late Princess Dewa-Ammajee. I have, &c.,

(Signed) G. F. EDMONSTONE,
Secretary to the Government of India.

The extract accompanying the above letter was as follows:

Extract from a Despatch from the Hon. Court of Directors, dated April 27, 1854; *No.* 16.

The claim of the Ex-Rajah to these promissory notes is wholly untenable. He assumes to be the heir to the Princess Dewa-Ammajee, who died at the commencement of the Coorg war, having been, as appears from Lieut.-General Cotton's letter of the 23rd September, 1853, put to death, with all her children, by the Rajah, a few days before the advance of our troops. Her effects, if they had rightfully devolved to him, were included in the general confiscation of his property, which took place at the conquest.

(Signed) G. F. EDMONSTONE.
Secretary to the Government of India.

It was on the 4th of April, 1837, that the Madras Government, in a letter addressed by its secretary to Messrs. Binny and Co., the Rajah's solicitors, *first* denied the proprietary claim of his Highness to the Government security standing in the name of the late Princess Dewa-Ammajee, *without, however, assigning any ground* upon which that denial rested. Now, the Rajah having been deposed in 1834, the atrocity he is accused of must have been committed prior to that time, and have been known to the Company before 1837. Why, then, did they not state the alleged crime as their reason for denying his claim in 1837? Why did they suppress all mention of it in the proclamation they issued upon declaring war against his Highness? Why did they not publish it to the world prior to 1854, that is, more than twenty years after it was said to have been committed. Why, but that they hoped the lapse of time might deprive their victim of every chance of exculpating himself from so diabolical a charge, all the witnesses who could have proved that the parties had died of cholera, being no longer in existence?

Nothing could exceed the Rajah's astonishment at having so monstrous a crime imputed to him; and accordingly, on the 23rd of November, 1854, he addressed the following letter, in reply, to G. F. Edmonstone, Esq., Secretary to the Government of India, Fort William, Calcutta:—

Sir,—I beg to acknowledge the receipt of your letter of the 30th of June, 1854, enclosing an extract from a despatch from the Honourable the Court of Directors, dated 27th April, 1854; and, as I have now appealed to the Courts of justice for redress, I forbear from noticing your communication further than by denying, with the greatest indignation and in the most positive terms, the calumny contained in the extract from the despatch, which states that I put the Princess Dewa Ammajee and her children to death—a calumny which has not the slightest foundation to rest upon, and the falsehood of which would be at once proved by inquiry.—I have, &c.,

(Signed) Veer Rajunder Wadeer.

November 23, 1854.

The second charge is contained in the following extract from a letter addressed to the Rajah of Coorg, by S. Græme, Esq., the Resident of Napoore, and dated November 6, 1833:—

"By the perpetration of murder, and the exercise of tyranny over your subjects, you will cause mismanagement in your kingdom: this does not become you, and you are recommended to refrain from such a course of conduct."

The Rajah replied to this communication, on the 10th of November, 1833, in these words:—

"The contents of your letter, dated the 6th inst., greatly

surprised me. You charge me with the diabolical crimes of murder and tyranny. *I beg of you to let me know the names of the parties I have put to death—the place—the date,* on which I am charged with the crimes alleged against me: then I shall be able to furnish you with full particulars and information."

On the 17th November, Mr. Græme answered as follows:—

Camp, Mysore, 17th November, 1833.

I am in receipt of your letter, and in reply, *after many humble apologies,* beg to state, *that it was the mistake of the translator. I do not bring such charges against you, and beg of you to forgive me.* What I meant was this: that you should prevent your officers from doing anything of the sort.[1]

An equally triumphant answer to a similar charge has been already given, by Mr. Jeaffreson, in the following words:—

"Another fact also, I think it my duty to state, in disproof of such calumnies. Before leaving Bombay (on a visit to the Rajah), several persons residing there, and who had received intelligence that some of their relations in Coorg had been unjustly and most cruelly put to death by the Rajah, desired me to make inquiries as to the truth of such reports. This I did; *and it was with the greatest pleasure I obtained the surest proof of the falsehood of such allegations, by the appearance before me, in real flesh and blood, of the very parties who were said to have been so unceremoniously disposed of.*"[2]

Had these charges against the Rajah, and particularly the dreadful one of sororicide, been founded in fact, would not, we repeat, the East India Company have gladly blazoned them to the world in their proclamation—that is, in their official apology for despoiling him of his throne and treasures? Instead, however, of their so doing, the only specific charge they

[1] The original letter is in the Rajah's possession.

[2] See page 40.

brought against him was that of refusing to deliver up Canara Menon, whose detention was fully justified by the law of nations.

As to the general accusations of cruelty and oppression, they come with an ill grace from those whose power has been cemented by blood, rapine, and corruption, and who, until very lately, have connived at the infliction of torture upon their unfortunate subjects.[1] *Quis tulerit Gracchos de seditione querentes?*

But even these shadowy and undefined charges are most satisfactorily disposed of by the memorial and statement inserted elsewhere, as well as by the testimony borne to the same effect by Mr. Jeaffreson.[2]

The truly flattering testimonials[3] given in favour of the Rajah's character and conduct, by Colonel Carpenter, Lord Ellenborough, and Lieut.-Colonel Macgregor—all of whom, from their having been on the spot, had ample opportunities of judging of the truth or falsehood of such allegations—furnish still further evidence in his behalf, and cannot fail to prove, to every unprejudiced and disinterested mind, the moral impossibility of his having been guilty of the foul crimes so falsely and cruelly attributed to him; for as easily might "the Ethiopian change his skin, or the leopard his spots," as a man who had steeped his hands in the blood of those nearest to him, could remain for years without betraying some indications of the ferocity natural to him, or evincing some symptoms of remorse for so dreadful a crime.

> "Quo semel imbuta est recens, servabit odorem
> Testa diu."

Ample time was given, before the Rajah's arrival in this country, for the *proofs*, had there been any, of such atrocious

[1] See, *Is the Practice of Torture in Madras with the Sanction of the Authorities of Leadenhall Street?* By Malcolm Lewin, Esq., &c., late Second Judge of Sudder and Foujdaree Adawlut of the Madras Presidency. 1856.

[2] See pages 40, 60, 61. [3] See pages 63, 64, 65.

crimes to have preceded him; but the cordial reception he met with from the Directors of the Honourable East India Company—the distinguished honour conferred upon him by her most gracious Majesty, who condescended to stand sponsor to his Highness's daughter, the Princess Gouramma, and to admit him to her levees and state balls—not less than the alacrity with which so many distinguished members of both Houses of Parliament came forward to advocate his cause against the Court of Directors—prove to demonstration that all the efforts of his traducers had failed in their effect, and that the character of his Highness had come forth, like gold from the fiery ordeal, with greater purity.

And now a word or two as to the origin and propagation of these wicked libels. In the year 1830, Mr. Casamajor, the Company's Resident at Mysore, having been sent on a mission to Coorg, behaved in so insolent and domineering a manner to the Rajah, that the latter, unable to brook such conduct, wrote to the Governor-General to desire that his agent might be recalled. The Local Government acquiesced, thereby acknowledging the justice of the Rajah's complaint; Mr. Casamajor was removed, and, shortly after his departure, the sinister reports in question were, for the first time, bruited abroad: with whom they originated it will not, therefore, be difficult to determine.

Two persons have been chiefly instrumental in circulating these reports—Thornton, the author of a history of British India, and an American missionary, rejoicing in the name of Mœgling. Repudiating, as we do, the remotest intention of imputing wrong motives to any one, yet, considering that it is the bounden duty of a writer, before he gives currency to reports seriously affecting the character of individuals, to satisfy himself as to their truth, we cannot but regret that Mr. Thornton should have brought against the Rajah charges, in support of which he has not adduced a single authority, not even the shadow of a proof. That Mr. Thornton did not take the trouble to make the requisite inquiry as to the correctness of his allegations, will, we apprehend, be sufficiently proved by the following passage from his work, and its refutation. "The annexation," he says, "of the conquered territory to the British dominions is not, on the first view, *so clearly justifiable*; but a very few words of explanation will show that, in this instance also, the right course was taken. *The Rajah was childless*, and he had taken effectual measures to cut off all pretensions to the succession not derived from himself. The vacant throne was without a claimant, and the power which had occupied the country was called upon to provide, in some manner, for the administration of the Government."[1] What will the reader think of the accuracy of the writer of the above passage when he is told that the Rajah of Coorg had, at the time of his deposal, a legitimate son, now living, and who, having been born in 1831, was two years old when the country was annexed?

The Rev. Mr. Mœgling, an American missionary, is the other person who has recently revived and given increased circulation to these calumnious reports, in his work entitled *Coorg Memoirs*, published at Bangalore in 1855. The malevolence and injustice which, as far as the Rajah is concerned, this reverend gentleman exhibits, is, indeed, painful in the extreme to every well-disposed and unprejudiced mind.

Mr. Mœgling, in his Preface,[2] observes—"A child of this house (the Rajah's family) has found her way into the Church of Christ; and Queen Victoria, Sovereign of the greatest empire of the world, has not been ashamed to bestow her name and affection upon a daughter of the last of the Haleri Rajahs. Auspicious omen for Coorg! O give thanks unto the Lord; for he is good; for his mercy endureth for ever!"

Now, let us ask, through whose instrumentality did the Church of England obtain this interesting neophyte, except through that of her father the Rajah, who, in bringing his

[1] *History of British India*, vol. v. p. 214.

[2] Page 5.

daughter to this country for the purpose of having her trained up in Christ's pure religion, must have acted either *proprio motu*, or under influence from above: if the former, he is surely deserving of commendation; if the latter, he is, at least, entitled to respect, as the recipient of divine grace. The terms, therefore, of *wretch, teller of barefaced lies, fool, and coward,* &c., heaped so unsparingly by this *Christian* missionary upon his Highness, are equally unbecoming the reverend author, either as a minister or a gentleman.

In the same page, Mr. Mœgling assures his readers that "no statement has been made without careful examination. Truth has been told *sine irâ et studio*"; and he then thus apostrophizes them—"Let such as know how to pray, offer up their supplications for the salvation of Coorg. The judgment of God has descended upon the race of the Rajahs!"

Now, had the Rev. Mr. Mœgling made the necessary inquiries as to the truth of the atrocious calumnies he was about to give such extensive circulation to, he would have learnt that the Rajah's sister and her family had been carried off by cholera; he must have known that Lord Ellenborough, Mr. Jeaffreson, Colonels Carpenter and Macgregor, had all borne testimony in the Rajah's favour; he could not have been ignorant of the regret expressed by the Rajah's subjects upon his being deposed, or of the gratuitous charge brought against him by Mr. Græme—a charge which that gentleman afterwards retracted, offering, at the same time, the amplest apology; and, lastly, the energy with which the Rajah's case was taken up by the House of Lords, and the cordial reception given to his Highness by the *élite* of the English aristocrary, must have come to his knowledge: all which circumstances the reverend missionary should have given publicity to, had he written, as he asserts he did, *sine irâ et studio*. Either, therefore, this reverend author, this preacher of the Gospel, never did make the careful examination which he assures his readers he did, or, having made it, he has suppressed the truth. We leave him the choice of either horn of the dilemma, with this friendly suggestion, that the next time he prays, it should be for a greater supply of Christian charity and love of truth, and for a mind more disposed to do justice between man and man.

As a further proof how little the assertions of this reverend gentleman are to be depended upon, we quote the following passages from his work :—

"The Government of the Company succeeded (the deposition of the Rajah), person and property were now safe, peace and security were established in Coorg."[1]

"Little or nothing has been done for the education of the people. Nothing has been attempted systematically to raise them in intelligence and character; on the contrary, it is a common complaint that three vices, *drunkenness, sexual licentiousness, and lying, have greatly increased during the Company's reign.* In former days the native rulers suppressed drunkenness by summary and violent means; now, the Government draws a large revenue from the sale of intoxicating liquors. Prostitutes formerly were turned out of the country, and Coorg men severely punished and degraded for intercourse with low-caste women; now, the wicked and shameless may do as they please. In past times, the Rajah would, now and then, cut off a man's tongue or his head, for having spoken a falsehood; in these days, the man who lies most impudently, and swears most fearlessly, often gains the cause: when lies do not succeed, bribes do."[2]

We certainly never expected to find, in a Christian minister, the most sacred duty of whose vocation is to inculcate truth, and promote charity and good will among men, so lamentable a discrepancy between acts and professions: and, after such a

[1] Page 206.

[2] Page 28.

specimen of what a missionary *ought not to be,* we trust that our American brethren will, in future, exercise greater care and circumspection in the choice of those upon whom they impose so awful and responsible a duty.

Our little narrative being now brought to a conclusion, the writer may be allowed to observe, that the objects of his work will be sufficiently attained, if, in addition to affording amusement and information, it shall cause the policy and acts of the Honourable East India Company to be watched with a more vigilant eye than heretofore, and shall awaken in the public mind a sympathy on behalf of the last of the Coorg Rajahs, his Highness Veer RajunderWadeer,—

"A MAN MORE SINN'D AGAINST, THAN SINNING."

THE END.